500⁺

Persian Phrases

Daily Conversations for Better Communication

Nazanin Mirsadeghi

Bahar Books

www.baharbooks.com

Mirsadeghi, Nazanin
    500+ Persian Phrases: Daily Conversations for Better Communication (Farsi-English Bi-lingual Edition)/
Nazanin Mirsadeghi

Editor: Molly Singleton-Coyne

1st Edition: ISBN-10: 1939099404 - ISBN-13: 978-1-939099-40-2

2nd Edition:
ISBN-10: 1939099463
ISBN-13: 978-1-939099-46-4

Copyright © 2014 by Bahar Books, LLC

Published by Bahar Books, White Plains, New York

Table of Contents

Preface

This book of **500+ *Persian Phrases*** contains common phrases that you can use during everyday conversation. The phrases in this book have been divided into more than 25 categories, such as: introductions, greetings, compliments, the weather, disappointments, preferences, likes, dislikes, goals & plans, apologies, invitations, consolations, measurements and descriptions. Each section consists of several dialogues and each phrase has been presented in two different formats: the written form and the spoken form. Since there are different dialects in different regions of Iran, it is important to note that the spoken phrases provided in this book are based on the dialect spoken in Tehran, the capital of Iran. To facilitate the learning process four different symbols have been assigned to indicate whether the phrase is written, spoken, formal or an idiom. All phrases are accompanied by their English translations; however, the English translations of the Persian phrases are not precise. The translations provided in this book for each Persian phrase are the closest to their equivalent phrase used in the English language. The phonetic transcription (transliteration) for each Persian phrase has been provided to help readers with pronunciation.

The book also provides essential information regarding the Persian alphabet and numbers, and the pronunciation of the Persian letters.

This book will serve as a reference for those who are learning the Persian language to help them advance their conversational language skills.

A special thanks to Molly Singleton-Coyne for her diligent work as the editor of this book.

Nazanin Mirsadeghi

Pronouncing Persian Letters – Table A

ă like the "a" in arm	* آ – ا
b like the "b" in boy	ب – بـ
p like the "p" in play	پ – پـ
t like the "t" in tree	ت – تـ
s like the "s" in sun	ث – ثـ
j like the "j" in jam	ج – جـ
č like the "ch" in child	چ – چـ
h like the "h" in hotel	ح – حـ
ǩ like "ch" in the German word *bach*, or Hebrew word *smach*.	خ – خـ
d like the "d" in door	د
z like the "z" in zebra	ذ
r like the "r" in rabbit	ر
z like the "z" in zebra	ز
ž like the "z" in zwago	ژ
s like the "s" in sun	س – سـ
š like the "sh" in shell	ش – شـ
s like the "s" in sun	ص – صـ
z like the "z" in zebra	ض – ضـ

t like the **"t"** in tree	ط
z like the **"z"** in zebra	ظ
ʻ is a glottal stop, like between the syllables of "uh-oh"	ع – ـع – ـعـ – عـ
ğ like the **"r "** in French word *merci*	غ – ـغ – ـغـ – غـ
f like the **"f "** in fall	ف – ـف
ğ like the **"r"** in French word *merci*	ق – ـق
k like the **"k"** in kite	ک – ـک
g like the **"g"** in game	گ – ـگ
l like the **"l"** in lost	ل – ـل
m like the **"m"** in master	م – ـمـ
n like the **"n"** in night	ن – ـنـ
v like the **"v"** in van	و
o like the **"o"** in ocean	و
On some occasions, it has no sound and becomes silent.	و
u like the **"u"** in sure	او – و *
h like the **"h"** in hotel	ه – ـه – ـهـ – هـ
e like the **"e"** in element	ه – ـه
y like the **"y"** in yellow	ی – ـیـ
I like the **"ee"** in need	ای – ی – ـیـ – ایـ*

* long vowels

a like the "a" in animal	‑ ‑ اَ **
o like the "o" in ocean	ُ ‑ اُ **
e like the "e" in element	‑ اِ **

** short vowels

Arabic Signs

Represents doubled consonants.	ّ
' is a glottal stop, like between the syllables of "uh‑oh".	ء
an like "an" in the "can"	ً

Persian Letters with the Same Pronunciation

(extracted from Table A)

t like the **"t"** in tree	ت – تـ
	ط
ğ like the **"r"** in French word *merci*	ق – قـ
	غ – غـ – ـفـ – ـغ
h like the **"h"** in hotel	ح – حـ
	ه – ـه – ـهـ – هـ
s like the **"s"** in sun	ث – ثـ
	س – سـ
	ص – صـ
z like the **"z"** in zebra	ذ
	ز
	ض – ضـ
	ظ

Names of Persian Letters- Table B

alef	آ– ا
be	ب – بـ
pe	پ – پـ
te	ت – تـ
se	ث – ثـ
jim	ج – جـ
če	چ – چـ
he	ح – حـ
ke	خ – خـ
dăl	د
zăl	ذ
re	ر
ze	ز
že	ژ
sin	س – سـ
šin	ش – شـ
săd	ص – صـ
zăd	ض – ضـ

tă	ط
ză	ظ
eyn	ع – ع – ع – ع
ğeyn	غ – غ – غ – غ
fe	ف – ف
ğăf	ق – ق
kăf	ک – ک
găf	گ – گ
lăm	ل – ل
mim	م – م
nun	ن – ن
văv	و
he	ه – ه – ه – ه
ye	ی – ی

Persian Numbers– Table C

English	Number	Persian Number	Persian
one	1	۱	یک
two	2	۲	دو
three	3	۳	سه
four	4	۴	چهار
five	5	۵	پنج
six	6	۶	شش
seven	7	۷	هفت
eight	8	۸	هشت
nine	9	۹	نه
ten	10	۱۰	ده
eleven	11	۱۱	یازده
twelve	12	۱۲	دوازده
thirteen	13	۱۳	سیزده
fourteen	14	۱۴	چهارده
fifteen	15	۱۵	پانزده
sixteen	16	۱۶	شانزده

seventeen	17	۱۷	هفده
eighteen	18	۱۸	هیجده
nineteen	19	۱۹	نوزده
twenty	20	۲۰	بیست
thirty	30	۳۰	سی
forty	40	۴۰	چهل
fifty	50	۵۰	پنجاه
sixty	60	۶۰	شصت
seventy	70	۷۰	هفتاد
eighty	80	۸۰	هشتاد
ninety	90	۹۰	نود
(one) hundred	100	۱۰۰	صد
two hundred	200	۲۰۰	دویست
three hundred	300	۳۰۰	سیصد
four hundred	400	۴۰۰	چهارصد
five hundred	500	۵۰۰	پانصد
six hundred	600	۶۰۰	ششصد
seven hundred	700	۷۰۰	هفتصد

eight hundred	800	۸۰۰	هشتصد
nine hundred	900	۹۰۰	نهصد
(one) thousand	1000	۱۰۰۰	هزار

Persian Pronouns- Table D

Plural	Singular
We = ما /mǎ/	**I** = من /man/
You = شُما /šo.mǎ/	**You** (informal) = تو /to/ **You** (formal) = شُما /šo.mǎ/
They = آنها /ǎn.hǎ/	**He – She / It** = او / آن /u/ - /ǎn/

Guide to the Symbols Used in this Book:

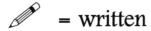 = written

= spoken

= formal

(i) = idioms, expressions, slang

Introductions

✏ : اسمِ شما چیست؟

/es.me- šo.mă- čist/

💬 : اسمِ شما چیه؟

/es.me- šo.mă- či.ye/

What is your name?

✏ : اسمِ من ساراست.

/es.me- man- să.răst/

💬 : اسمِ من ساراس.

/es.me- man- să.răs/

My name is Sara.

🖋 ✏ : نامِ خانوادگیِ شما چیست؟

/nă.me- ǩă.ne.vă.de.gi.ye- šo.mă- čist/

💬 : فامیلی تون چیه؟

/fă.mi.li.tun- či.ye/

What is your last name?

✏ 💬 : صمیمی.

/sa.mi.mi/

Samimi.

✏️ : از آشنایی با شما خوشوقتم.

/az- ăš.nă.yi- bă- šo.mă- ǩoš.vaǧ.tam/

💬 : از آشنایی تون خوشوقتم.

/az- ăš.nă.yi.tun- ǩoš.vaǧ.tam/

It is nice to meet you.

💬 ✏️ : من هم همینطور.

/man- ham- ha.min.tor/

You too.

✏️ : قیافه ی شما برایم خیلی آشناست!

/ǧi.yă.fe.ye- šo.mă- ba.ră.yam- ǩey.li- ă.še.năst/

💬 : قیافَتون برام خیلی آشناس!

/ǧi.yă.fa.tun- ba.răm- ǩey.li- ăš.năs/

You look so familiar!

✏️ : من خواهر لیلا هستم.

/man- ǩă.ha.re- ley.lă- has.tam/

💬 : من خواهر لیلام.

/man- ǩă.ha.re- ley.lăm/

I am Leila's sister.

✏️ : ببخشید، من شما را قبلاً کجا دیده ام؟

/be.baǩ.šid- man- šo.mă- ră- ǧab.lan- ko.jă- di.de.am/

💬 : ببخشید، من شما رو قبلاً کجا دیدم؟

/be.baǩ.šid- man- šo.mă- ro- ǧab.lan- ko.jă- di.dam/

Excuse me. Have we met before?

✏️ : نمی دانم. من همسایه ی رایان هستم.

/ne.mi.dă.nam- man- ham.să.ye.ye- ră.yăn- has.tam/

💬 : نمی دونم. من همسایه ی رایانم.

/ne.mi.du.nam- man- ham.să.ye.ye- ră.yă.nam/

I don't know. I am Ryan's neighbor.

ببخشید، ما قبلاً همکار نبودیم؟ : ✏️ 💬

/be.bak̆.šid- mǎ- ğab.lan- ham.kǎr- na.bu.dim/

Excuse me. Didn't we work together?

فکر نمی کنم. : ✏️ 💬

/fekr- ne.mi.ko.nam/

I don't think so.

سلام، شما مریم هستید، مگر نه؟ : ✏️

/sa.lǎm- šo.mǎ- mar.yam- has.tid- ma.gar- na/

سلام، شما مریم هستین، مگه نه؟ : 💬

/sa.lǎm- šo.mǎ- mar.yam- has.tin- ma.ge- na/

Hi. You are Maryam, aren't you?

بله. ولی من متأسّفانه شما را به جا نمی آورم. : ⓘ ✏️

/ba.le- va.li- man- mo.te.'as.se.fǎ.ne- šo.mǎ- rǎ- be- jǎ- ne.mi.ǎ.va.ram/

بله. ولی من متأسّفانه شما رو به جا نمیارم. : ⓘ 💬

/ba.le- va.li- man- mo.te.'as.se.fǎ.ne- šo.mǎ- ro- be- jǎ- ne.mi.yǎ.ram/

Yes, but unfortunately I don't remember you.

ما پارسال در مهمانیِ سینا با هم آشنا شدیم. : ✏️

/mǎ- pǎr.sǎl- dar- meh.mǎ.ni.ye- si.nǎ- bǎ- ham- ǎ.še.nǎ- šo.dim/

ما پارسال توی مهمونیِ سینا با هم آشنا شدیم. : 💬

/mǎ- pǎr.sǎl- tu.ye- meh.mu.ni.ye- si.nǎ- bǎ- ham- ǎš.nǎ- šo.dim/

We met last year at Sina's party.

حالا شما را شناختم. شما همکلاسیِ سینا هستید. : ✏️

/hǎ.lǎ- šo.mǎ- rǎ- še.nǎk̆.tam- šo.mǎ- ham.ke.lǎ.si.ye- si.nǎ- has.tid/

حالا شناختَمتون. شما همکلاسیِ سینا هستین. : 💬

/hǎ.lǎ- še.nǎk̆.ta.me.tun- šo.mǎ- ham.ke.lǎ.si.ye- si.nǎ- has.tin/

Now I recognize you! You are Sina's classmate.

✏️ : بله. درست است. شما هم دخترخاله ی سینا هستید، مگر نه؟

/ba.le- do.rost- ast- šo.mǎ- ham- doǩ.tar- ǩǎ.le.ye- si.nǎ- has.tid- ma.gar- na/

💬 : بله. درسته. شما هم دخترخاله ی سینا هستین، مگه نه؟

/ba.le- do.ros.te- šo.mǎ- ham- doǩ.tar- ǩǎ.le.ye- si.nǎ- has.tin- ma.ge- na/

Yes. That's correct; and you are his cousin, right?

✏️ : نه. من دوستِ سینا هستم.

/na- man- dus.te- si.nǎ- has.tam/

💬 : نه. من دوستِ سینام.

/na- man- dus.te- si.nǎm/

No. I am Sina's friend.

✏️ : سلام، می خواهَم خانمَم، سارا را به شما معرّفی کنم.

/sa.lǎm- mi.ǩǎ.ham- ǩǎ.no.mam- sǎ.rǎ- rǎ- be- šo.mǎ- mo.'ar.re.fi- ko.nam/

💬 : سلام، می خوام خانمَم، سارا رو به شما معرّفی کنم.

/sa.lǎm- mi.ǩǎm- ǩǎ.no.mam- sǎ.rǎ- ro- be- šo.mǎ- mo.'ar.re.fi- ko.nam/

Hello. I want to introduce my wife Sara to you.

✏️ : سلام. تعریفِ شما را خیلی شنیده ایم!

/sa.lǎm- ta'.ri.fe- šo.mǎ- rǎ- ǩey.li- še.ni.de.im/

💬 : سلام. تعریفِ شما رو خیلی شنیدیم!

/sa.lǎm- ta'.ri.fe- šo.mǎ- ro- ǩey.li- še.ni.dim/

Hello. We heard so many good things about you!

Personal Information

✏️ : شما اهل کجا هستید؟

/šo.mǎ- ah.le- ko.jǎ- has.tid/

💬 : شما اهل کجایین؟

/šo.mǎ- ah.le- ko.jǎ.yin/

Where are you from?

✏️ : من اهل تهران هستم.

/man- ah.le- teh.rǎn- has.tam/

💬 : من اهل تهرانَم.

/man- ah.le- teh.rǎ.nam/

I am from Tehran.

✏️ : شما مال کدام کشور هستید؟

/šo.mǎ- mǎ.le- ko.dǎm- keš.var- has.tid/

💬 : شما مال کدوم کشورین؟

/šo.mǎ- mǎ.le- ko.dum- keš.va.rin/

What country do you come from?

✏️💬 : ایران.

/i.rǎn/

Iran.

✏️ : شما کجایی هستید؟

/šo.mǎ- ko.jǎ.yi- has.tid/

💬 : شما کجایی هستین؟

/šo.mǎ- ko.jǎ.yi- has.tin/

Where are you from?

✏️ : من ایرانی هستم.

/man- i.rǎ.ni- has.tam/

💬 : من ایرانیَم.

/man- i.rǎ.ni.yam/

I am Iranian.

✏️ : چه زبان هایی بلدید؟

/če- za.bǎn.hǎ.yi- ba.la.did/

💬 : چه زبونایی بلدین؟

/če- za.bu.nǎ.yi- ba.la.din/

What languages do you speak?

✏️💬 : فارسی، انگلیسی و اسپانیایی.

/fǎr.si- en.ge.li.si- va- es.pǎ.ni.yǎ.yi/

Persian, English and Spanish.

✏️ : چند زبان بلدید؟

/čand- za.bǎn- ba.la.did/

💬 : چندتا زبون بلدین؟

/čand- tǎ- za.bun- ba.la.din/

How many languages do you speak?

✏️ : من پنج زبان می دانم.

/man- panj- za.bǎn- mi.dǎ.nam/

💬 : من پنج تا زبون می دونم.

/man- panj- tǎ- za.bun- mi.du.nam/

I speak five languages.

✎ : ملّیت شما چیست؟

/mel.li.ya.te- šo.mă- čist/

💬 : ملّیت تون چیه؟

/mel.li.ya.te.tun- či.ye/

What is your nationality?

✎ : من آمریکایی هستم.

/man- ăm.ri.kă.yi- has.tam/

💬 : من آمریکایی ام.

/man- ăm.ri.kă.yi.am/

I am American.

✎ : مذهب شما چیست؟

/maz.ha.be- šo.mă- čist/

💬 : مذهب تون چیه؟

/maz.ha.be.tun- či.ye/

What is you religion?

✎ : من مسیحی / کلیمی / مسلمان هستم.

/man- ma.si.hi- ka.li.mi- mo.sal.măn- has.tam/

💬 : من مسیحی / کلیمی / مسلمونَم.

/man- ma.si.hi- ka.li.mi- mo.sal.mu.nam/

I am Christian/ Jewish/ Muslim.

✎ : شغل شما چیست؟

/šoğ.le- šo.mă- čist/

💬 : شغل شما چیه؟

/šoğ.le- šo.mă- či.ye/

What is your occupation?

✎ : من کارمند بانک هستم.

/man- kăr.man.de- bănk- has.tam/

💬 : من کارمند بانکم.

/man- kăr.man.de- băn.kam/

I am a bank clerk.

شما کجا کار می کنید؟ : ✏️

/šo.mǎ- ko.jǎ- kǎr- mi.ko.nid/

شما کجا کار می کنین؟ : 💬

/šo.mǎ- ko.jǎ- kǎr- mi.ko.nin/

Where do you work?

من در اداره ی پُست کار می کنم. : ✏️

/man- dar- e.dǎ.re.ye- post- kǎr- mi.ko.nam/

من توی اداره ی پُست کار می کنم. : 💬

/man- tu.ye- e.dǎ.re.ye- post- kǎr- mi.ko.nam/

I work at the post office.

شما چطور؟ شما کارتان چیست؟ : ✏️

/šo.mǎ- če.tor- šo.mǎ- kǎ.re.tǎn- čist/

شما چطور؟ شما کارتون چیه؟ : 💬

/šo.mǎ- če.tor- šo.mǎ- kǎ.re.tun- či.ye/

How about you? What do you do?

من دانشجو هستم. : ✏️

/man- dǎ.neš.ju- has.tam/

من دانشجو ام. : 💬

/man- dǎ.neš.ju.am/

I am a college student.

چه می خوانید؟ چه رشته ای؟ : ✏️

/če- mi.ǩǎ.nid- če- reš.te.i/

چی می خوونین؟ چه رشته ای؟ : 💬

/či- mi.ǩu.nin- če- reš.te.i/

What do you study? What is your field?

اقتصاد. : 💬 ✏️

/eǧ.te.sǎd/

Economics.

✐ : کدام دانشگاه؟

/ko.dăm- dă.neš.găh/

💬 : کدوم دانشگاه؟

/ko.dum- dă.neš.găh/

Which university?

💬 ✐ : دانشگاه کلمبیا.

/dă.neš.gă.he- ko.lom.bi.yă/

Columbia University.

💬 ✐ : چه مقطعی؟ لیسانس یا فوق لیسانس؟

/če- mağ.ta.ʿi- li.săns- yă- fo.ğe.li.săns/

What level? Undergraduate or graduate?

💬 ✐ : دکترا.

/dok.to.ră/

Ph.D.

✐ : کارِ شما چیست؟

/kă.re- šo.mă- čist/

💬 : کارِتون چیه؟

/kă.re.tun- či.ye/

What type of business are you in?

✐ : کارم تجارتِ فرش است.

/kă.ram- te.jă.ra.te- farš- ast/

💬 : کارم تجارتِ فرشه.

/kă.ram- te.jă.ra.te- far.še/

I trade rugs.

🖉 : شما چند سال تان است؟

/šo.mắ- čand- sǎ.le.tǎn- ast/

💬 : شما چند سال تونه؟

/šo.mǎ- čand- sǎ.le.tu.ne/

How old are you?

🖉 : من بیست و هشت سالَم است.

/man- bis.to- hašt- sǎ.lam- ast/

💬 : من بیست و هشت سالَمه.

/man- bis.to- hašt- sǎ.la.me/

I'm twenty eight years old.

🖉 : متولّد چه سالی هستید؟

/mo.te.val.le.de- če- sǎ.li- has.tid/

💬 : متولّد چه سالی هستین؟

/mo.te.val.le.de- če- sǎ.li- has.tin/

In what year were you born?

🖉 : من متولّد سال ۱۹۶۷ میلادی هستم.

/man- mo.te.val.le.de- sǎ.le- he.zǎ.ro- noh.sa.do- šas.to- haf.te- mi.lǎ.di- has.tam/

💬 : من متولّد سال ۱۹۶۷ میلادیَم.

/man- mo.te.val.le.de- sǎ.le- he.zǎ.ro- noh.sa.do- šas.to- haf.te- mi.lǎ.di.yam/

I was born in 1967.

🖉 : شما مجرّد هستید؟

/šo.mǎ- mo.jar.rad- has.tid/

💬 : شما مجرّدین؟

/šo.mǎ- mo.jar.ra.din/

Are you single?

🖉 : بله. مجرّد هستم.

/ba.le- mo.jar.rad- has.tam/

💬 : بله. مجرّدم.

/ba.le- mo.jar.ra.dam/

Yes. I am single.

شما متأهّل هستید؟ : ✏️

/šo.mă- mo.te.'ah.hel- has.tid/

شما متأهّل هستین؟ : 💬

/šo.mă- mo.te.'ah.hel- has.tin/

Are you married?

نه، امّا نامزد دارم. : 💬 ✏️

/na- am.mă- năm.zad- dă.ram/

No, but I'm engaged.

این آقا شوهر شماست؟ : ✏️ 👔

/in- ă.ğă- šo.ha.re- šo.măst/

این آقا شوهرِ شماس؟ : 💬 👔

/in- ă.ğă- šo.ha.re- šo.măs/

Is this gentleman your husband?

نه. شوهر سابقم است. طلاق گرفته ایم. : ✏️

/na- šo.ha.re- să.be.ğam- ast- ta.lăğ- ge.ref.te.im/

نه. شوهر سابقَمه. طلاق گرفتیم. : 💬

/na- šo.ha.re- să.be.ğa.me- ta.lăğ- ge.ref.tim/

No. He is my ex–husband. We are divorced.

شما بچّه دارید؟ : ✏️

/šo.mă- bač.če- ham- dă.rid/

شما بچّه دارین؟ : 💬

/šo.mă- bač.če- ham- dă.rin/

Do you have children?

بله، دوتا. یک پسر وَ یک دختر. : ✏️

/ba.le- do.tă- yek- pe.sar- va- yek- dok.tar/

بله، دوتا. یه پسر و یه دختر. : 💬

/ba.le- do.tă- ye- pe.sa.ro- ye- dok.tar/

Yes. I have two, a boy and a girl.

Greetings

✏️ 💬 : سلام! صبح بخیر!

/sa.lăm- sobh- be.ǩeyr/

Hello! Good morning!

✏️ 💬 : عصر بخیر!

/ʿasr- be.ǩeyr/

Good afternoon!

✏️ 💬 : شب بخیر!

/šab- be.ǩeyr/

Good night!

✏️ 💬 : صبحِ شما هم بخیر!

/sob.he- šo.mă- ham- be.ǩeyr/

Good morning to you too!

✏️ 💬 : عصرِ شما هم بخیر!

/ʿas.re- šo.mă- ham- be.ǩeyr/

Good afternoon to you too!

✏️ 💬 : شبِ شما هم بخیر!

/ša.be- šo.mă- ham- be.ǩeyr/

Good night to you too!

✐ : **روزتان بخیر!**

/ru.ze.tăn- be.ǩeyr/

💬 : **روزتون بخیر!**

/ru.ze.tun- be.ǩeyr/

Have a nice day!

✐ 💬 : **روزِ شما هم بخیر!**

/ru.ze- šo.mă- ham- be.ǩeyr/

Same to you too!

✐ : **روزِ خوبی داشته باشید!**

/ru.ze- ǩu.bi- dăš.te- bă.šid/

💬 : **روزِ خوبی داشته باشین!**

/ru.ze- ǩu.bi- dăš.te- bă.šin/

Have a good day!

✐ 💬 : **شما هم همینطورا!**

/šo.mă- ham- ha.min.tor/

You too!

✐ : **حالتان چطور است؟ خوبید؟**

/hă.le.tăn- če.tor- ast- ǩu.bid/

💬 : **حالتون چطوره؟ خوبین؟**

/hă.le.tun- če.to.re- ǩu.bin/

How are you? Are you o.k.?

✐ 💬 : **مرسی. خوبم.**

/mer.si- ǩu.bam/

Thanks. I'm fine.

خانواده خوبند؟ : ✎

/kǎ.ne.vǎ.de- ǩu.band/

خانواده خوبن؟ : 💬

/kǎ.ne.vǎ.de- ǩu.ban/

Is everything o.k. with your family?

بد نیستند. : ✎

/bad- nis.tand/

بد نیستن. : 💬

/bad- nis.tan/

They are o.k.

همه چیز خوب است؟ : ✎

/ha.me- čiz- ǩub- ast/

همه چیز خوبه؟ : 💬

/ha.me- čiz- ǩu.be/

Everything is fine?

بله. همه چیز خوب خوب است. : ✎

/ba.le͞- ha.me- čiz- ǩu.be- ǩub- ast/

آره. همه چیز خوب خوبه. : 💬

/ǎ.re- ha.me- čiz- ǩu.be- ǩu.be/

Yes. Everything is just fine.

اوضاع و احوالَت روبراه است؟ : ✎

/o.zǎ ʼ- va- ah.vǎ.lat- ru.be.rǎh- ast/

اوضاع و احوالت روبراهه؟ : 💬

/o.zǎ.ʼo͞- ah.vǎ.let- ru.be.rǎ.he/

Everything is going well with you?

بله. شکایتی نیست. : ✎

/ba.le- še.kǎ.ya.ti- nist/

بله. شکایتی نیس. : 💬

/ba.le- še.kǎ.ya.ti- nis/

Yes. Can't complain!

کجایی؟ پیدایَت نیست. : ✎

/ko.jă.yi- pey.dă.yat- nist/

کجایی؟ پیدات نیس. : 💬

/ko.jă.yi- pey.dăt- nis/

Where have you been hiding?

این روزها سرم خیلی شلوغ است. : ✎

/in- ruz.hă- sa.ram- ǩey.li- šo.luǧ- ast/

این روزا سرم خیلی شلوغه. : 💬

/in- ruză- sa.ram- ǩey.li- šo.lu.ǧe/

I am very busy these days.

تازه چه خبر؟ : ✎ 💬

/tă.ze- če- ǩa.bar/

What's new?

خبرِ تازه ای نیست. سلامتی. : ✎

/ǩa.ba.re- tă.ze.i- nist- sa.lă.ma.ti/

خبرِ تازه ای نیس. سلامتی. : 💬

/ǩa.ba.re- tă.ze.i- nis- sa.lă.ma.ti/

Nothing's new. All is well.

از سارا خبری داری؟ : ✎ 💬

/az- să.ră- ǩa.ba.ri- dă.ri/

Have you heard anything from Sara?

نه. هیچ خبری ندارم. خیلی وقت است از او بی خبرم. : ✎

/na- hič- ǩa.ba.ri- na.dă.ram- ǩey.li- vaǧt- ast- az- u- bi.ǩa.ba.ram/

نه. هیچ خبری ندارم. خیلی وقته ازَش بی خبرم. : 💬

/na- hič- ǩa.ba.ri- na.dă.ram- ǩey.li- vaǧ.te- a.zaš- bi.ǩa.ba.ram/

No, nothing. I haven't heard from her in a long time.

✎ : از طرف من به همه سلام برسان.

/az- ta.ra.fe- man- be- ha.me- sa.lăm- be.re.san/

💬 : از طرف من به همه سلام برسون.

/az- ta.ra.fe- man- be- ha.me- sa.lăm- be.re.sun/

Say hello to everyone for me.

✎ 💬 : حتماً. تو هم همینطور.

/hat.man- to- ham- ha.min.tor/

Sure. You too.

Hospitalities

✏ : خوش آمدید!

/ǩoš- ǎ.ma.did/

💬 : خوش اومدین!

/ǩoš- u.ma.din/

Welcome to our house!

💬 ✏ : ممنونم.

/mam.nu.nam/

Thank you.

✏ 💬 ⚷ : مشتاقِ دیدارِ !

/moš.tǎ.ǧe- di.dǎr/

I am excited to see you!

✏ 💬 ⚷ : به همچنین.

/be- ham.če.nin/

Same here.

خواهش می کنم تشریف بیاورید تو! : 🖊️ 👤

/ǩǎ.heš- mi.ko.nam- taš.rif- bi.yǎ.va.rid- tu/

خواهش می کنم تشریف بیارین تو! : 💬 👤

/ǩǎ.heš- mi.ko.nam- taš.rif- bi.yǎ.rin- tu/

Please come in.

کفش هایم را در بیاورم؟ : 🖊️

/kafš.hǎ.yam- rǎ- dar- bi.yǎ.va.ram/

کفشامو در بیارم؟ : 💬

/kafš.hǎ.mo- dar- bi.yǎ.ram/

Should I take my shoes off?

بله. ممنون می شوم، اگر اشکالی ندارد. : 🖊️

/ba.le- mam.nun- mi.ša.vam- a.gar- eš.kǎ.li- na.dǎ.rad/

بله. ممنون می شم، اگه اشکالی نداره. : 💬

/ba.le- mam.nun- mi.šam- a.ge- eš.kǎ.li- na.dǎ.re/

Yes. I'd appreciate it, if you don't mind.

هیچ اشکالی ندارد. : 🖊️

/hič- eš.kǎ.li- na.dǎ.rad/

هیچ اشکالی نداره. : 💬

/hič- eš.kǎ.li- na.dǎ.re/

No problem.

بفرمایید بنشینید! : 🖊️ 👤

/be.far.mǎ.yid- ben.ši.nid/

بفرمایین بشینین! : 💬 👤

/be.far.mǎ.yin- be.ši.nin/

Please have a seat!

مرسی. : 💬 🖊️

/mer.si/

Thank you.

نوشیدنی چه میل دارید، چای بیاورم خدمتِ تان یا قهوه؟ : ✏️ 👔

/nu.ši.da.ni- če- meyl- dă.rid- čăy- bi.yă.va.ram- ǩed.ma.te.tăn- yă- ğah.ve/

نوشیدنی چی میل دارین، چایی بیارم خدمتِ تون یا قهوه؟ : 💬 👔

/nu.ši.da.ni- či- meyl- dă.rin- čă.yi- bi.yă.ram- ǩed.ma.te.tun- yă- ğah.ve/

What can I offer you to drink? May I serve you tea or coffee?

زحمتِ تان نمی دهم. چند دقیقه بیشتر نمی توانم بمانم. : ✏️ 👔

/zăh.ma.te.tăn- ne.mi.da.ham- čand- da.ği.ǧe- biš.tar- ne.mi.ta.vă.nam- be.mă.nam/

زحمتِ تون نمی دم. چند دقیقه بیشتر نمی توونم بمونم. : 💬 👔

/zăh.ma.te.tun- ne.mi.dam- čand- da.ği.ǧe- biš.tar- ne.mi.tu.nam- be.mu.nam/

I won't trouble you. I can stay only for a few minutes.

زحمت نیست. چای یا قهوه؟ هردوشان حاضرست. : ✏️ 👔

/zăh.mat- nist- čăy- yă- ğah.ve- har- do.šăn- hă.zer- ast/

زحمت نیس. چایی یا قهوه؟ هردوتاش حاضره. : 💬 👔

/zăh.mat- nis- čă.yi- yă- ğah.ve- har- do.tăš- hă.ze.re/

No trouble. Tea or coffee? Both are ready.

قهوه، لطفاً. : 💬 ✏️

/ğah.ve- lot.fan/

Coffee, please.

شکر هم داخلَش بریزم؟ : ✏️

/še.kar- ham- dă.ǩe.laš- be.ri.zam/

شکرَم توش بریزم؟ : 💬

/še.ka.ram- tuš- be.ri.zam/

Should I add sugar?

نه، مرسی. : 💬 ✏️

/na- mer.si/

No, thanks.

✏️ 💬 : شیر چطور؟

/šir- če.tor/

How about milk?

✏️ : پودرِ شیر دارید؟

/pud.re- šir- dǎ.rid/

💬 : پودرِ شیر دارین؟

/pud.re- šir- dǎ.rin/

Do you have any (powdered) coffee creamer?

✏️ 💬 : نه. متأسّفانه ندارم.

/na- mo.te.ʾas.se.fǎ.ne- na.dǎ.ram/

No. I'm sorry I don't.

✏️ 💬 : پس تلخ می خورم.

/pas- talx̌- mi.ǩo.ram/

I'll have it black then.

✏️ 🧁 : لطفاً از خودتان پذیرایی کنید! بفرمایید شیرینی میل کنید!

/lot.fan- az- ǩo.de.tǎn- pa.zi.rǎ-yi- ko.nid- be.far.mǎ.yid- ši.ri.ni- meyl- ko.nid/

🧁 💬 : لطفاً از خودتون پذیرایی کنین! بفرمایین شیرینی میل کنین!

/lot.fan- az- ǩo.de.tun- pa.zi.rǎ-yi- ko.nin- be.far.mǎ.yin- ši.ri.ni- meyl- ko.nin/

Please help yourself! Have some cookies (pastries)!

✏️ 💬 🧁 : چَشم. حتماً می خورم.

/čašm- hat.man- mi.ǩo.ram/

Sure. I will.

✏️ : خیلی خوشحالم کردید که آمدید.

/ǩey.li- ǩoš.hǎ.lam- kar.did- ke- ǎ.ma.did/

💬 : خیلی خوشحالم کردین که اومدین.

/ǩey.li- ǩoš.hǎ.lam- kar.din- ke- u.ma.din/

I am so glad that you came.

✏️ : من هم از دیدنِ تان خیلی خوشحال شدم.

/man- ham- az- di.da.ne.tǎn- ǩey.li- ǩoš.hǎl- šo.dam/

💬 : منَم از دیدنِ تون خیلی خوشحال شدم.

/ma.nam- az- di.da.ne.tun- ǩey.li- ǩoš.hǎl- šo.dam/

I was happy to see you too.

37

Health & Well-Being

✏️ : حالَت چطورست؟

/hǎ.lat- če.to.rast/

💬 : حالت چطوره؟

/hǎ.let- če.to.re/

How are you feeling?

💬 ✏️ : خوبم. ممنون.

/ǩu.bam- mam.nun/

I am fine. Thanks.

✏️ : حالتان بهترست؟

/hǎ.le.tǎn- beh.ta.rast/

💬 : حالتون بهتره؟

/hǎ.le.tun- beh.ta.re/

Do you feel better?

💬 ✏️ : بهترم، مرسی.

/beh.ta.ram- mer.si/

I'm better. Thanks.

حالا بهتر شده اید؟ : ✐

/hă.lă- beh.tar- šo.de.id/

حالا بهتر شدین؟ : 💬

/hă.lă- beh.tar- šo.din/

Are you better now?

نه. هنوز مریضم. : 💬 ✐

/na- ha.nuz- ma.ri.zam/

No. I am still sick.

سرماخوردگی تان برطرف شد؟ : 🛒 ✐

/sar.mă.ǩor.de.gi.tăn- bar.ta.raf- šod/

سرماخوردگی تون برطرف شد؟ : 🛒 💬

/sar.mă.ǩor.de.gi.tun- bar.ta.raf- šod/

Is your cold gone?

بله. خوشبختانه زود برطرف شد. : 💬 ✐

/ba.le- ǩoš.baǩ.tă.ne- zud- bar.ta.raf- šod/

Yes. Fortunately it went away quickly.

تب هم داری؟ : ✐

/tab- ham- dă.ri/

تبَم داری؟ : 💬

/ta.bam- dă.ri/

Do you have a fever too?

بله. تبَم خیلی بالاست. : ✐

/ba.le- ta.bam- ǩey.li- bă.lăst/

آره. تبَم خیلی بالاس. : 💬

/ă.re- ta.bam- ǩey.li- bă.lăs/

Yes. I have a high fever.

✏️ : سرِتان هنوز درد می کند؟

/sa.re.tăn- ha.nuz- dard- mi.ko.nad/

💬 : سرِتون هنوز درد می کنه؟

/sa.re.tun- ha.nuz- dard- mi.ko.ne/

Do you still have a headache?

✏️ : بله. سردردم بدتر هم شده است.

/ba.le- sar.dar.dam- bad.tar- ham- šo.de- ast/

💬 : بله. سردردم بدترَم شده.

/ba.le- sar.dar.dam- bad.ta.ram- šo.de/

Yes. My headache has gotten worse.

Compliments

✏️ 💬 : سارا خودتی؟

/să.ră- ǩo.de.ti/

Sara, is that you?

✏️ : بله. خودم هستم!

/ba.le- ǩo.dam- has.tam/

💬 : آره. خودِ خودَمَم!

/ă.re- ǩo.de- ǩo.da.mam/

Yes. It's me!

✏️ : اصلاً عوض نشده ای!

/as.lan- 'a.vaz- na.šo.de.i/

💬 : اصلاً عوض نشدی!

/as.lan- 'a.vaz- na.šo.di/

You haven't changed a bit!

💬 ✏️ : مرسی. تو هم همینطور.

/mer.si- to- ham- ha.min.tor/

Thanks. Neither have you.

چقدر خوشگل شده ای! : 🖉

/če.ğadr- ǩoš.gel- šo.de.i/

چقدر خوشگل شدی! : 💬

/če.ğadr- ǩoš.gel- šo.di/

You look so beautiful!

ممنونم. : 💬 🖉

/mam.nu.nam/

Thank you.

چقدر لباسَت قشنگ است! : 🖉

/če.ğadr- le.bǎ.sat- ğa.šang- ast/

چقدر لباست قشنگه! : 💬

/če.ğadr- le.bǎ.set- ğa.šan.ge/

What a beautiful dress you are wearing!

مرسی. امروز آن را خریده ام! : 🖉

/mer.si- em.ruz- ǎn- rǎ- ǩa.ri.de.am/

مرسی. امروز خریدمش! : 💬

/mer.si- em.ruz- ǩa.ri.da.meš/

Thanks. I bought it today!

مویَت خیلی خوب شده است! : 🖉

/mu.yat- ǩey.li- ǩub- šo.de- ast/

موت خیلی خوب شده! : 💬

/mut- ǩey.li- ǩub- šo.de/

You hair looks very nice!

تازه رنگ کرده ام. : 🖉

/tǎ.ze- rang- kar.de.am/

تازه رنگ کردم. : 💬

/tǎ.ze- rang- kar.dam/

I've had it dyed recently.

✏ ⓘ : چقدر این رنگ به تو می آید!

/če.ğadr- in- rang- be- to- mi.ă.yad/

💬 ⓘ : چقدر این رنگ بهت میاد!

/čĕ.ğadr- in- rang- be.het- mi.yăd/

This color suits you very well!

✏ : مرسی، قرمز، رنگ مورد علاقه ی من است.

/mer.si- ğer.mez- ran.ge- mo.re.de- ʾa.lă.ğe.ye- man- ast/

💬 : مرسی، قرمز، رنگ مورد علاقمه.

/mer.si- ğer.mez- ran.ge- mo.re.de- ʾa.lă.ğa.me/

Thanks. Red is my favorite color.

✏ : بَه بَه، چه خانه ی قشنگی دارید!

/bah- bah- če- kă.ne.ye- ğa.šan.gi- dă.rid/

💬 : بَه بَه، چه خونه ی قشنگی دارین!

/bah- bah- če- ku.ne.ye- ğa.šan.gi- dă.rin/

Wow, what a beautiful house you have!

✏ : بزرگ نیست، امّا خیلی نورگیر است.

/bo.zorg- nist- am.mă- key.li- nur.gir- ast/

💬 : بزرگ نیس، امّا خیلی نورگیره.

/bo.zorg- nis- am.mă- key.li- nur.gi.re/

It's not big, but it has a lot of natural light!

✏ : چقدر باسلیقه خانه تان را تزئین کرده اید!

/če.ğadr- bă.sa.li.ğe- kă.ne.tăn- ră- taz.ʾin- kar.de.id/

💬 : چقدر باسلیقه خونه تونو تزئین کردین!

/če.ğadr- bă.sa.li.ğe- ku.na.tu.no- taz.ʾin- kar.din/

How tastefully you've decorated your house!

✏ : من رشته ی دکوراسیون داخلی خوانده ام.

/man- reš.te.ye- de.ko.ră.si.yo.ne- dă.ke.li- kăn.de.am/

💬 : من رشته ی دکوراسیون داخلی خووندم.

/man- reš.te.ye- de.ko.ră.si.yo.ne- dă.ke.li- kun.dam/

I studied Interior Design in college.

43

✏️ ⓘ : از هر پنجه تان صد هنر می ریزد!

/az- har- pan.je.tăn- sad- ho.nar- mi.ri.zad/

💬 ⓘ : از هر پنجه تون صدتا هنر می ریزه!

/az- har- pan.ja.tun- sad.tă- ho.nar- mi.ri.ze/

You have so many skills!

✏️ 👔 : لطف دارید.

/lotf- dă.rid/

💬 👔 : لطف دارین.

/lotf- dă.rin/

You're being kind.

✏️ : عجب صدای فوق العاده ای دارید!

/ˈa.jab- se.dă.ye- fo.ğol.ˈă.de.i- dă.rid/

💬 : عجب صدای فوق العاده ای دارین!

/ˈa.jab- se.dă.ye- fo.ğol.ˈă.de.i- dă.rin/

What an amazing voice you have!

✏️ 👔 : نظر لطف تان است!

/na.za.re- lot.fe.tăn- ast/

💬 👔 : نظر لطف تونه!

/na.za.re- lot.fe.tu.ne/

That's very kind of you!

✏️ ⓘ : دست پخت تان حرف ندارد!

/dast- poǩ.te.tăn- harf- na.dă.rad/

💬 ⓘ : دست پخت تون حرف نداره!

/dast- poǩ.te.tun- harf- na.dă.re/

Your cooking is undoubtedly amazing!

✏️ : متشکّرم. خوشحالم که خوش تان آمده است.

/mo.te.šak.ke.ram- ǩoš.hă.lam- ke- ǩo.še.tăn- ă.ma.de- ast/

💬 : متشکّرم. خوشحالم خوش تون اومده.

/mot.šak.ke.ram- ǩoš.hă.lam- ǩo.še.tun- u.ma.de/

Thank you. I am so flattered to hear that.

✏️ : سارا خیلی آدمِ باملاحظه ای ست.

/să.ră- ǩey.li- ă.da.me- bă.mo.lă.he.ze.ist/

💬 : سارا خیلی آدمِ باملاحظه ایه.

/să.ră- ǩey.li- ă.da.me- bă.mo.lă.he.ze.i.ye/

Sara is a very considerate person.

✏️ : آره. کاملاً درست می گویی.

/ă.re- kă.me.lan- do.rost- mi.gu.yi/

💬 : آره. کاملاً درست می گی.

/ă.re- kă.me.lan- do.rost- mi.gi/

Yes. You are absolutely right.

✏️ : همسایه هایِتان چطورند؟

/ham.să.ye.hă.ye.tăn- če.to.rand/

💬 : همسایه هاتون چطورن؟

/ham.să.ye.hă.tun- če.to.ran/

How are our neighbors?

✏️ : آره. آدم هایِ بسیار خوبی هستند.

/ă.re- ă.dam.hă.ye- bes.yăr- ǩu.bi- has.tand/

💬 : آره. آدمای خیلی خوبی هستن.

/ă.re- ă.damă.ye- ǩey.li- ǩu.bi- has.tan/

Yes. They are very good people.

🎙️ 💬 ✏️ : من خیلی به شما ارادت دارم.

/man- ǩey.li- be- šo.mă- e.ră.dat- dă.ram/

I am very fond of you.

🎙️ 💬 ✏️ : به همچنین.

/be- ham.če.nin/

Likewise.

✏️ : سخنرانی ات عالی بود!

/so.ǩan.ră.ni.at- 'ǎ.li- bud/

💬 : سخنرانیت عالی بود!

/so.ǩan.ră.nit- 'ǎ.li- bud/

Your speech was excellent!

✏️ : ممنون. رویَش خیلی کار کرده بودم.

/mam.nun- ru.yaš- ǩey.li- kǎr- kar.de- bu.dam/

💬 : ممنون. روش خیلی کار کرده بودم.

/mam.nun- ruš- ǩey.li- kǎr- kar.de- bu.dam/

Thank you. I worked very hard on it.

✏️ : دخترَت خیلی خوش پوش است!

/doǩ.ta.rat- ǩey.li- ǩoš.puš- ast/

💬 : دخترت خیلی خوش پوشه!

/doǩ.ta.ret- ǩey.li- ǩoš.pu.še/

Your daughter is very fashionable!

✏️ ℹ️ : آره، به خودَش می رسد.

/ǎ.re- be- ǩo.daš- mi.re.sad/

ℹ️ 💬 : آره، به خودش می رسه.

/ǎ.re- be- ǩo.deš- mi.re.se/

Yes, she takes care of her appearance.

Weather

✎ : هوا چطورست؟

/ha.vă- če.tor- ast/

💬 : هوا چطوره؟

/ha.vă- če.to.re/

How is the weather?

✎ : هوا عالی است.

/ha.vă- 'ă.li- ast/

💬 : هوا عالیه.

/ha.vă- 'ă.li.ye/

It is great.

✎ 💬 : چه هوای خوبی!

/če- ha.vă.ye- ǩu.bi/

What nice weather!

✎ : آره. محشر است!

/ă.re- mah.šar- ast/

💬 : آره. محشره!

/ă.re- mah.ša.re/

Yes. It's fantastic.

✎ : چه نسیم خوبی می آید!

/če- na.si.me ̱- k̆u.bi- mi.ǎ.yad/

💬 : چه نسیم خوبی میاد!

/če- na.si.me ̱- k̆u.bi- mi.yǎd/

What a nice breeze!

✎ : نسیم بهاری است!

/na.si.me ̱- ba.hǎ.ri- ast/

💬 : نسیم بهاریه!

/na.si.me ̱- ba.hǎ.ri.ye/

It's the springtime breeze.

✎ : درخت ها همه سبز شده اند.

/de.rak̆t.hǎ- ha.me- sabz- šo.de.and/

💬 : درختا همه سبز شدن.

/de.rak̆.tǎ- ha.me- sabz- šo.dan/

The trees have all turned green.

✎ : درخت ها دارند شکوفه می کنند.

/de.rak̆t.hǎ- dǎ.rand- šo.ku.fe- mi.ko.nand/

💬 : درختا دارن شکوفه می کنن.

/de.rak̆.tǎ- dǎ.ran- šo.ku.fe- mi.ko.nan/

The trees are blooming.

ⓘ ✎ : دارد مثل سیل باران می بارد.

/dǎ.rad- mes.le- seyḻ- bǎ.rǎn- mi.bǎ.rad/

ⓘ 💬 : داره مثل سیل بارون میاد.

/dǎ.re- mes.le- seyḻ- bǎ.run- mi.yǎd/

It's raining like crazy.

✎ : باران که بند آمد، می رویم بیرون.

/bǎ.rǎn- ke- band- ǎ.mad- mi.ra.vim- bi.run/

💬 : بارون که بند اومد، می ریم بیرون.

/bǎ.run- ke- band- u.mad- mi.rim- bi.run/

When it stops raining, we will go out.

✏️ : عجب رنگین کمان قشنگی!

/'a.jab- ran.gin- ka.mǎ.ne- ǧa.šan.gi/

💬 : عجب رنگین کمون قشنگی!

/'a.jab- ran.gin- ka.mu.ne- ǧa.šan.gi/

What a beautiful rainbow!

✏️ : من عاشق رنگین کمانم!

/man- 'ǎ.še.ǧe- ran.gin- ka.mǎ.nam/

💬 : من عاشق رنگین کمونم!

/man- 'ǎ.še.ǧe- ran.gin- ka.mu.nam/

I love rainbows!

✏️💬 : چه باد وحشتناکی!

/če- bǎ.de- vah.šat.nǎ.ki/

What a horrible wind!

✏️ : گردبادست.

/gerd.bǎ.dast/

💬 : گردباده.

/gerd.bǎ.de/

It's a tornado!

✏️ : صدای رعد را شنیدی؟

/se.dǎ.ye- ra'd- rǎ- še.ni.di/

💬 : صدای رعدو شنیدی؟

/se.dǎ.ye- ra'.do- še.ni.di/

Did you hear the thunder?

✏️ : فکر می کنم می خواهد توفان شود.

/fekr- mi.ko.nam- mi.ǩǎ.had- tu.fǎn- be.ša.vad/

💬 : فکر کنم می خواد توفان بشه.

/fekr- ko.nam- mi.ǩǎd- tu.fǎn- be.še/

I think it's going to turn into a storm.

هوا عجب سوزی دارد! : ✏️

/ha.vă- 'a.jab- su.zi- dă.rad/

هوا عجب سوزی داره! : 💬

/ha.vă- 'a.jab- su.zi- dă.re/

What a chilling wind!

بله. واقعاً سرد است. : ✏️

/ba.le- vă.ğe.'an- sard- ast/

بله. واقعاً سرده. : 💬

/ba.le- vă.ğe.'an- sar.de/

Yes. It's really cold.

چه برفِ بی موقعی! : 💬 ✏️

/če- bar.fe- bi.mo.ğe.' i/

What an untimely snow fall!

بله. این وقت سال دیگر نباید برف بیاید. : ✏️

/ba.le- in- vağ.te- săl- di.gar- na.bă.yad- barf- bi.yă.yad/

بله. این وقت سال دیگه نباید برف بیاد. : 💬

/ba.le- in- vağ.te- săl- di.ge- na.bă.yad- barf- bi.yăd/

Yes. It shouldn't snow at this time of the year.

از سرما جانم به لبم رسیده است! : ✏️ ⓘ

/az- sar.mă- jă.nam- be- la.bam- re.si.de- ast/

از سرما جونم به لبم رسیده! : 💬 ⓘ

/az- sar.mă- ju.nam- be- la.bam- re.si.de/

I'm sick of the cold weather!

من هم همینطور. : 💬 ✏️

/man- ham- hamin.tor/

Me too.

✏ : این زمستان لعنتی هم که تمام نمی شود!

/in- ze.mes.tă.ne- laʼ.na.ti- ham- ke- ta.măm- ne.mi.ša.vad/

💬 : این زمستون لعنتی هم که تموم نمی شه!

/in- ze.mes.tu.ne- laʼ.na.ti- ham- ke- ta.mum- ne.mi.še/

This damn winter doesn't want to end!

✏ : من که دیگر تحمّل سرما را ندارم!

/man- ke- di.gar- ta.ham.mo.le- sar.mă- ră- na.dă.ram/

💬 : من که دیگه تحمّل سرما رو ندارم!

/man- ke- di.ge- ta.ham.mo.le- sar.mă- ro- na.dă.ram/

I can't stand the cold weather any more!

✏ : تابستان داغی در پیش داریم!

/tă.bes.tă.ne- dă.ği- dar- piš- dă.rim/

💬 : تابستون داغی در پیش داریم!

/tă.bes.tu.ne- dă.ği- dar- piš- dă.rim/

We have a hot summer ahead of us!

✏ : آره. امّا بچّه ها کیف می کنند.

/ă.re- am.mă- bač.če.hă- keyf- mi.ko.nand/

💬 : آره. امّا بچّه ها کیف می کنن.

/ă.re- am.mă- bač.če.hă- keyf- mi.ko.nan/

Yes, but kids will have a blast!

✏ 💬 : از گرما کلافه شدیم!

/az- gar.mă- ka.lă.fe- šo.dim/

We are so frustrated because of the heat!

✏ : آره. این گرما غیرقابلِ تحمّل است.

/ă.re- in- gar.mă- ğey.re- ğă.be.le- ta.ham.mol - ast/

💬 : آره. این گرما غیرقابلِ تحمّله.

/ă.re- in- gar.mă- ğey.re- ğă.be.le- ta.ham.mo.le/

Yes. This heat is unbearable.

از آن آفتاب های تندست! : 🖉

/az- ăn- ăf.tăb.hă.ye-tond- ast/

از اون آفتابای تنده! : 💬

/az- un- ăf.tă.bă.ye- ton.de/

It's one of those hot sunny days!

این آفتاب جان می دهد برای رفتن کنار آب! : 🖉 ⓘ

/in- ăf.tăb- jăn- mi.da.had- ba.ră.ye- raf.tan- ke.nă.re- ăb/

این آفتاب جون می ده واسه رفتن کنارِ آب! : 💬 ⓘ

/in- ăf.tăb- jun- mi.de- vă.se- raf.tan- ke.nă.re- ăb/

This sun calls for a day on the beach!

امسال از باران خبری نیست. : 🖉

/em.săl- az- bă.răn- ǩa.ba.ri- nist/

امسال از بارون خبری نیس. : 💬

/em.săl- az- bă.run- ǩa.ba.ri- nis/

There is no sign of rain this year.

ممکن است خشکسالی بشود. : 🖉

/mom.ken- ast- ǩošk.să.li- be.ša.vad/

ممکنه خشکسالی بشه. : 💬

/mom.ke.ne- ǩošk.să.li- be.še/

It might turn into a drought.

گول ظاهر آفتابی اش را نخور! : 🖉

/gu.le- ză.he.re- ăf.tă.bi.aš- ră- na.ǩor/

گول ظاهر آفتابیش رو نخور! : 💬

/gu.le- ză.he.re- ăf.tă.biš- ro- na.ǩor/

Don't let its sunny look fool you!

درست می گویی. هنوز سردست. : 🖉

/do.rost- mi.gu.yi- ha.nuz- sard- ast/

درست می گی. هنوز سرده. : 💬

/do.rost- mi.gi- ha.nuz- sar.de/

You are right. It's still cold.

امسال ما آب وَ هوای خوبی داشتیم. : ✎

/em.săl- mă- ăb- va- ha.vă.ye- ǩu.bi- dăš.tim/

امسال ما آب و هوای خوبی داشتیم. : 💬

/em.săl- mă- ă.bo- ha.vă.ye- ǩu.bi- dăš.tim/

We had it good this year.

ما برعکس، زمستان خیلی سختی را گذراندیم. : ✎

/mă- bar.'aks- ze.mes.tă.ne- ǩey.li- saǩ.ti- ră- go.za.răn.dim/

ما برعکس، زمستون خیلی سختی رو گذروندیم. : 💬

/mă- bar.'aks- ze.mes.tu.ne- ǩey.li- saǩ.ti- ro- go.za.run.dim/

On the contrary. We had a very difficult winter this year.

عجب پائیز دلگیری شده است! : ✎

/'a.jab- pă.'i.ze- del.gi.ri- šo.de- ast/

عجب پاییز دلگیری شده! : 💬

/'a.jab- pă.'i.ze- del.gi.ri- šo.de/

What a gloomy autumn!

به خاطر ابری بودن هواست. : ✎

/be- ǩă.te.re- ab.ri- bu.da.ne- ha.văst/

به خاطر ابری بودن هواس. : 💬

/be- ǩă.te.re- ab.ri- bu.da.ne- ha.văs/

It's because of the cloudy weather.

نگاه کن! برگ درخت ها همه ریخته است! : ✎

/ne.găh- kon- bar.ge- de.raǩt.hă- ha.me- riǩ.te- ast/

نگا کن! برگ درختا همه ریخته! : 💬

/ne.gă- kon- bar.ge- de.raǩ.tă- ha.me- riǩ.te/

Look! The leaves have all fallen.

آره. دیروز شدیداً باد می آمد. : ✎

/ă.re- di.ruz- ša.di.dan- băd- mi.ă.mad/

آره. دیروز شدیداً باد میومد. : 💬

/ă.re- di.ruz- ša.di.dan- băd- mi.yu.mad/

Yes. It was very windy yesterday.

Goals & Plans

✏️ : امسال تابستان کجا می روی؟

/em.săl- tă.bes.tăn- ko.jă- mi.ra.vi/

💬 : امسال تابستون کجا می ری؟

/em.săl- tă.bes.tun- ko.jă- mi.ri/

Where are you going this summer?

✏️ : می خواهم به اسپانیا بروم.

/mi.kă.ham- be- es.pă.ni.yă- be.ra.vam/

💬 : می خوام برم اسپانیا.

/mi.kăm- be.ram- es.pă.ni.yă/

I want to go to Spain.

✏️ : کی فارغ التّحصیل می شوی؟

/key- fă.re.ğot.tah.sil- mi.ša.vi/

💬 : کی فارغ التّحصیل می شی؟

/key- fă.re.ğot.tah.sil- mi.ši/

When are you going to graduate?

✏️ : امیدوارم بتوانم امسال فارغ التّحصیل شوم.

/o.mid.vă.ram- be.ta.vă.nam- em.săl- fă.re.ğot.tah.sil- ša.vam/

💬 : امیدوارم بتوونم امسال فارغ التّحصیل بشم.

/o.mid.vă.ram- be.tu.nam- em.săl- fă.re.ğot.tah.sil- be.šam/

I hope I can graduate this year.

دوست داری کجای دنیا را ببینی؟ : ✎

/dust- dă.ri- ko.jă.ye- don.yă- ră- be.bi.ni/

دوس داری کجای دنیا رو ببینی؟ : 💬

/dus- dă.ri- ko.jă.ye- don.yă- ro- be.bi.ni/

What part of the world would you like to see?

آرزو دارم یک روز به آفریقا سفر کنم. : ✎

/ă.re.zu- dă.ram- yek- ruz- be- ăf.ri.ğă- sa.far- ko.nam/

آرزو دارم یه روزی یه سفر برم آفریقا. : 💬

/ă.re.zu- dă.ram- ye- ru.zi- ye- sa.far- be.ram- ăf.ri.ğă/

I dream about traveling to Africa one day.

از شغلَت راضی هستی؟ : ✎

/az- šoğ.lat- ră.zi- has.ti/

از شغلت راضی هستی؟ : 💬

/az- šoğ.let- ră.zi- has.ti/

Are you happy with your job?

نه. قصد دارم شغلَم را عوض کنم. : ✎

/na- ğasd- dă.ram- šoğ.lam- ră- 'a.vaz- ko.nam/

نه. قصدم اینه که شغلَمو عوض کنم. : 💬

/na- ğas.dam- i.ne- ke- šoğ.la.mo- 'a.vaz- ko.nam/

No. I intend to change my job.

می خواهی آپارتمان بخری؟ : ✎

/mi.ḱă.hi- ă.păr.te.măn- be.ḱa.ri/

می خوای آپارتمان بخری؟ : 💬

/mi.ḱăy- ă.păr.te.măn- be.ḱa.ri/

Do you want to buy an apartment?

نه. هدفم این است که تا سال دیگر خانه بخرم. : ✎

/na- ha.da.fam- in- ăst- ke- tă- să.le- di.gar- ḱă.ne- be.ḱa.ram/

نه. هدفم اینه که تا سال دیگه خونه بخرم. : 💬

/na- ha.da.fam- i.ne- ke- tă- să.le- di.ge- ḱu.ne- be.ḱa.ram/

No. My goal is to buy a house by next year.

چقدر محّل کارَت به خانه ات نزدیک است! : ✏

/če.ğadr- ma.hal.le- kǎ.rat- be- kǎ.ne.at- naz.dik- ast/

چقدر محّل کارت به خونَت نزدیکه! : 💬

/če.ğadr- ma.hal.le- kǎ.ret- be- ku.nat- naz.di.ke/

Your work is so close to your house!

آره. خیال دارم ماشینَم را بفُروشم. : ✏

/ǎ.re- ǩi.yǎl- dǎ.ram- mǎ.ši.nam- rǎ- be.fo.ru.šam/

آره. خیال دارم ماشینَمو بفروشم. : 💬

/ǎ.re- ǩi.yǎl- dǎ.ram- mǎ.ši.na.mo- bef.ru.šam/

Yes. I am thinking of selling my car.

قصد سفر داری؟ : ✏ 💬

/ğas.de- sa.far- dǎ.ri/

Are you planning to travel?

آره. تصمیم گرفته ام به دیدن خواهرم بروم. : ✏

/ǎ.re- tas.mim- ge.ref.te.am- be- di.da.ne- kǎ.ha.ram- be.ra.vam/

آره. تصمیم گرفتم برم دیدن خواهرم. : 💬

/ǎ.re- tas.mim- ge.ref.tam- be.ram- di.da.ne- kǎ.ha.ram/

Yes. I have decided to visit my sister.

تا به حال ندیده بودم آدامس بجَوی! : ✏

/tǎ- be.hǎl- na.di.de- bu.dam- ǎ.dǎms- be.ja.vi/

تا حالا ندیده بودم آدامس بجویی! : 💬

/tǎ- hǎ.la- na.di.de- bu.dam- ǎ.dǎms- be.jo.yi/

I've never seen you chewing gum!

دارم سعی می کنم سیگار را ترک کنم. : ✏

/dǎ.ram- sa'y- mi.ko.nam- si.ğǎr- rǎ- tark- ko.nam/

دارم سعی می کنم سیگارو ترک کنم. : 💬

/dǎ.ram- sa'y- mi.ko.nam- si.ğǎ.ro- tark- ko.nam/

I am trying to quit smoking.

کالیفرنیا را دوست داشتی؟ : 🖋

/kǎ.li.for.ni.yǎ- rǎ- dust- dǎš.ti/

کالیفرنیا رو دوس داشتی؟ : 💬

/kǎ.li.for.ni.yǎ- ro- dus- dǎš.ti/

Did you like California?

خیلی. برنامه ام این است که تا آخرِ سال به کالیفرنیا مهاجرت کنم . : 🖋

/key.li- bar.nǎ.me.am- in- ast- ke- tǎ- ǎ.ǩa.re- sǎl- be- kǎ.li.for.ni.yǎ- mo.hǎ.je.rat- ko.nam/

خیلی. برنامم اینه که تا آخرِ سال مهاجرت کنم برم کالیفرنیا. : 💬

/key.li- bar.nǎ.mam- i.ne- ke- tǎ- ǎ.ǩa.re- sǎl- mo.hǎ.je.rat- ko.nam- be.ram- kǎ.li.for.ni.yǎ/

Very much. My plan is to move to California by the end of the summer.

می خواهی عربی یاد بگیری؟ : 🖋

/mi.ǩǎ.hi- ʻa.ra.bi- yǎd- be.gi.ri/

می خوای عربی یاد بگیری؟ : 💬

/mi.ǩǎy- ʻa.ra.bi- yǎd- be.gi.ri/

Do you want to learn Arabic?

نه، به سرم زده است فارسی یاد بگیرم. : 🖋 ⓘ

/na- be- sa.ram- za.de- ast- fǎr.si- yǎd- be.gi.ram/

نه، به سرم زده فارسی یاد بگیرم. : 💬 ⓘ

/na- be- sa.ram- za.de- fǎr.si- yǎd- be.gi.ram/

No. I'm thinking about learning Persian.

Disappointments

‎/ka.rat- če.to.rast/
‎کارَت چطورست؟ : ✏️

‎/ka.ret- če.to.re/
‎کارِت چطوره؟ : 💬

How is work?

‎/kǎ.ram- ǩey.li- es.te.res- dǎ.rad/
‎کارم خیلی استرس دارد. : ✏️

‎/kǎ.ram- ǩey.li- es.te.res- dǎ.re/
‎کارم خیلی استرس داره. : 💬

My work is very stressful.

‎/če.rǎ- in.ǧadr- ǎ.šof.te.i/
‎چرا اینقدر آشفته ای؟ : 💬 ✏️

Why are you so anxious?

‎/az- pa.se- kǎr.hǎ- bar.ne.mi.ǎ.yam/
‎از پسِ کارها بر نمی آیم. : ⓘ ✏️

‎/az- pa.se- kǎ.rǎ- bar.ne.mi.yǎm/
‎از پسِ کارا بر نمیام. : ⓘ 💬

I can't seem to manage things.

✎ : بنظر خیلی خسته می آیی!
/be.na.zar- ǩey.li- ǩas.te- mi.ǎ.yi/

💬 : بنظر خیلی خسته میای!
/be.na.zar- ǩey.li- ǩas.te- mi.yǎy/

You seem very tired!

✎ : این پروژه ی تازه خیلی پر دردسرست.
/in- pe.ro.je.ye- tǎ.ze- ǩey.li- por.dar.de.sa.rast/

💬 : این پروژه ی تازه خیلی پر دردسره.
/in- pe.ro.je.ye- tǎ.ze- ǩey.li- por.dar.de.sa.re/

This new project is a lot of work.

✎ 💬 : سرحال نیستی!
/sar.hǎl- nis.ti/

You don't seem to be in a good mood!

✎ : تحقیقم به جایی نرسیده است.
/tah.ǧi.ǧam- be- jǎ.yi- na.re.si.de- ast/

💬 : تحقیقم به جایی نرسیده.
/tah.ǧi.ǧam- be- jǎ.yi- na.re.si.de/

My research has gotten nowhere.

✎ : این کیک را تو پخته ای؟
/in- keyk- rǎ- to- poǩ.te.i/

💬 : این کیکو تو پختی؟
/in- key.ko- to- poǩ.ti/

Did you bake this cake?

✎ ⓘ : آره، امّا این دفعه خوب از آب در نیامده است.
/ǎ.re- am.mǎ- in- daf.'e- ǩub- az- ǎb- dar- na.yǎ.ma.de- ast/

💬 ⓘ : آره، امّا این دَفه خوب از آب در نیومده.
/ǎ.re- am.mǎ- in- da.fe- ǩub- az- ǎb- dar- na.yu.ma.de/

Yes, but it didn't turn out well this time.

ما دست پخت شما را خیلی دوست داریم! : ✎

/mǎ- dast- poǩ.te- šo.mǎ- rǎ- ǩey.li- dust- dǎ.rim/

ما دست پخت تونو خیلی دوس داریم! : 💬

/mǎ- dast- poǩ.te.tu.no- ǩey.li- dus- dǎ.rim/

We love your cooking very much.

مرسی، امّا برنجَم شفته شده است. : ✎

/mer.si- am.mǎ- be.ren.jam- šef.te- šo.de- ast/

مرسی، امّا برنجَم شفته شده. : 💬

/mer.si- am.mǎ- be.ren.jam- šef.te- šo.de/

Thanks but my rice is overcooked.

می آیی برویم سینما؟ : ✎

/mi.ǎ.yi- be.ra.vim- si.ne.mǎ/

میای بریم سینما؟ : 💬

/mi.yǎy- be.rim- si.ne.mǎ/

Should we go to the movies?

نه. سر کار گیر کرده ام. : ✎

/na- sa.re- ǩǎr- gir- kar.de.am/

نه. سر کار گیر کردم. : 💬

/na- sa.re- ǩǎr- gir- kar.dam/

No. I'm stuck at work.

رنگ مویَت را عوض کرده ای؟ : ✎

/ran.ge- mu.yat- rǎ- 'a.vaz- kar.de.i/

رنگ موت رو عوض کردی؟ : 💬

/ran.ge- mut- ro- 'a.vaz- kar.di/

Have you changed your hair color?

آره، امّا آنجور که می خواستم نشد! : ✎

/ǎ.re- am.mǎ- ǎn.jur- ke- mi.ǩǎs.tam- na.šod/

آره. امّا اونجوری که می خواستم نشد! : 💬

/ǎ.re- am.mǎ- un.ju.ri- ke- mi.ǩǎs.tam- na.šod/

Yes, but it didn't turn out the way I wanted.

هتل تان چطور بود؟ : ✏
/ho.te.le.tăn- če.tor- bud/

هتل تون چطور بود؟ : 💬
/ho.te.le.tun- če.tor- bud/

How was your hotel?

به آن تمیزی که فکر می کردیم نبود. : ✏
/be- ăn- ta.mi.zi- ke- fekr- mi.kar.dim- na.bud/

به اون تمیزی که فکر می کردیم نبود. : 💬
/be- un- ta.mi.zi- ke- fekr- mi.kar.dim- na.bud/

It was not as clean as we thought it would be.

صبحانه هم می دادند؟ : ✏
/sob.hă.ne- ham- mi.dă.dand/

صبحونه هم می دادن؟ : 💬
/sob.hu.ne- ham- mi.dă.dan/

Was breakfast included?

نه. شامل صبحانه نمی شد. : ✏
/na- šă.me.le- sob.hă.ne- ne.mi.šod/

نه. شامل صبحونه نمی شد. : 💬
/na- šă.me.le- sob.hu.ne- ne.mi.šod/

No. Breakfast was not included.

فیلمی که دیدید خوب بود؟ : ✏
/fil.mi- ke- di.did- ǩub- bud/

فیلمی که دیدین خوب بود؟ : 💬
/fil.mi- ke- di.din- ǩub- bud/

Was the movie you saw good?

بد نبود، امّا توقّع داشتیم بهتر از اینها باشد. : ✏
/bad- na.nud- am.mă- ta.vağ.ğo'- dăš.tim- beh.tar- az- in.hă- bă.šad/

بد نبود، امّا توقّع داشتیم بهتر از اینا باشه. : 💬
/bad- na.nud- am.mă- ta.vağ.ğo'- dăš.tim- beh.tar- az- i.nă- bă.še/

It was o.k., but we expected it to be much better.

61

✏️ : موضوعَش جالب نبود؟

/mo.zu.ʼaš- jă.leb- na.bud/

💬 : موضوعش جالب نبود؟

/mo.zu.ʼeš- jă.leb- na.bud/

Wasn't the story interesting?

✏️ : موضوعَش تازه نبود.

/mo.zu.ʼaš- tă.ze- na.bud/

💬 : موضوش تازه بود.

/mo.zuš- tă.ze- na.bud/

The story was not original.

✏️ : آپارتمانی را که برای فروش بود دیدی؟

/ă.păr.te.mă.ni- ră- ke- ba.ră.ye- fo.ruš- bud- di.di/

💬 : آپارتمانی رو که برای فروش بود دیدی؟

/ă.păr.te.mă.ni- ro- ke- ba.ră.ye- fo.ruš- bud- di.di/

Did you see the apartment that was for sale?

✏️ : آره، ولی داخل آپارتمان اصلاً به اندازه ی خارجَش جالب نبود.

/ă.re- va.li- dă.ke.le- ă.păr.te.măn- as.lan- be- an.dă.ze.ye- kă.re.jaš- jă.leb- na.bud/

💬 : آره، ولی توی آپارتمان اصلاً به اندازه ی بیرونش جالب نبود.

/ă.re- va.li- tu.ye- ă.păr.te.măn- as.lan- be- an.dă.ze.ye- bi.ru.neš- jă.leb- na.bud/

Yes, but the inside of the apartment was not as appealing as its outside.

✏️ : کلاس فارسی ات چطورست؟

/ke.lă.se- făr.si.at- če.to.rast/

💬 : کلاس فارسیت چطوره؟

/ke.lă.se- făr.sit- če.to.re/

How is your Farsi class?

✏️ : بد نیست، امّا این کلاس از آنی که فکر می کردم سخت ترست.

/bad- nist- am.mă- in- ke.lăs- az- ă.ni- ke- fekr- mi.kar.dam- sakt.ta.rast/

💬 : بد نیس، امّا این کلاس از اونی که فکر می کردم سخت تره.

/bad- nis- am.mă- in- ke.lăs- az- u.ni- ke- fekr- mi.kar.dam- sakt.ta.re/

Not bad, but this class is harder than I thought.

✏️ : دوچرخه ات را وصل کردی؟

/do.čar.ǩe.at- rǎ- vasl- kardi/

💬 : دوچرخَت رو وصل کردی؟

/do.čar.ǩat- ro- vasl- kardi/

Did you assemble your bicycle?

✏️ : نه. مگر به این سادگی هاست!

/na- ma.gar- be- in- sǎ.de.gi.hǎst/

💬 : نه. مگه به این سادگیاس!

/na- ma.ge- be- in- sǎ.de.gi.yǎst/

No. It's not that easy!

✏️💬 : اسکی یاد گرفتی؟

/es.ki- yǎd- ge.ref.ti/

Did you learn how to ski?

✏️ : هنوز نه. انتظار نداشتم به این سختی باشد.

/ha.nuz- na- en.te.zǎr- na.dǎš.tam- be- in- saǩ.ti- bǎ.šad/

💬 : هنوز نه. انتظار نداشتم به این سختی باشه.

/ha.nuz- na- en.te.zǎr- na.dǎš.tam- be- in- saǩ.ti- bǎ.še/

Not yet. I didn't expect it to be so difficult.

✏️ : تعمیرات خانه تان تمام شد؟

/ta'.mi.rǎ.te- ǩǎ.ne.tǎn- ta.mǎm- šod/

💬 : تعمیرات خونه تون تموم شد؟

/ta'.mi.rǎ.te- ǩu.na.tun- ta.mum- šod/

Is the renovation of your house finished?

ⓘ ✏️ : آره، ولی پدرمان درآمد تا تمام شد!

/ǎ.re- vali- pe.da.re.mǎn- dar- ǎ.mad- tǎ- ta.mǎm- šod/

ⓘ 💬 : آره، ولی پدرمون در اومد تا تموم شد!

/ǎ.re- vali- pe.da.re.mun- dar- u.mad- tǎ- ta.mum- šod/

Yes, but we had a hell of a time before it was done!

63

دندانَت را کشیدی؟ : ✏
/dan.dă.nat- ră- ke.ši.di/

دندونت رو کشیدی؟ : 💬
/dan.du.net- ro- ke.ši.di/

Did you get your tooth pulled?

کشیدم، امّا دخلم آمد! : ✏ ⓘ
/ke.ši.dam- am.mă- daǩ.lam- ă.mad/

کشیدم، امّا دخلم اومد! : 💬 ⓘ
/ke.ši.dam- am.mă- daǩ.lam- u.mad/

Yes, I did, but I went to hell and back!

کار دادگاهَت به کجا کشیده است؟ : ✏
/kă.re- dăd.gă.hat- be- ko.jă- ke.ši.de- ast/

کار دادگاهت به کجا کشیده؟ : 💬
/kă.re- dăd.gă.het- be- ko.jă- ke.ši.de/

How is it going with your case in court?

حالا حالاها ادامه دارد! : ✏
/hă.lă- hă.lă.hă- e.dă.me- dă.rad/

حالا حالاها ادامه داره! : 💬
/hă.lă- hă.lă.hă- e.dă.me- dă.re/

It will go on for a long time.

اتاق بچّه ها را تصفیه کردی؟ : ✏
/o.tă.ğe- bač.če.hă- ră- tas.fi.ye- kar.di/

اتاق بچّه ها رو تصفیه کردی؟ : 💬
/o.tă.ğe- bač.če.hă- ro- tas.fi.ye- kar.di/

Did you clean out the kids' room?

تقریباً. مگر تمام می شود! : ✏
/tağ.ri.ban- ma.gar- ta.măm- mi.ša.vad/

تقریباً. مگه تموم می شه! : 💬
/tağ.ri.ban- ma.ge- ta.mum- mi.še/

Almost. It never ends!

می خواهی در این رستوران ناهار بخوریم؟ : 🖉

/mi.ǩǎ.hi- dar- in- res.tu.rǎn- nǎ.hǎr- be.ǩo.rim/

می خوای توی این رستوران ناهار بخوریم؟ : 💬

/mi.ǩǎy- tu.ye- in- res.tu.rǎn- nǎ.hǎr- be.ǩo.rim/

Do you want to eat in this restaurant?

نه. غذای این رستوران زیاد جالب نیست. : 🖉

/na- ğa.zǎ.ye- in- res.tu.rǎn- zi.yǎd- jǎ.leb- nist/

نه. غذای این رستوران زیاد جالب نیس. : 💬

/na- ğa.zǎ.ye- in- res.tu.rǎn- zi.yǎd- jǎ.leb- nis/

No. The food in this restaurant is not that good.

توانستی وام بانکی بگیری؟ : 🖉

/ta.vǎ.nes.ti- vǎ.me- bǎn.ki- be.gi.ri/

توونستی وام بانکی بگیری؟ : 💬

/tu.nes.ti- vǎ.me- bǎn.ki- be.gi.ri/

Were you able to get a bank loan?

نه. خیلی به آن امید بسته بودم! : 🖉 ⓘ

/na- ǩey.li- be- ǎn- o.mid- bas.te- bu.dam/

نه. خیلی بهش امید بسته بودم! : 💬 ⓘ

/na- ǩey.li- be.heš- o.mid- bas.te- bu.dam/

No, and I really had my hopes up.

پسرَت مسابقه را بُرد یا باخت؟ : 🖉

/pe.sa.rat- mo.sǎ.be.ğe- rǎ- bord- yǎ- bǎǩt/

پسرت مسابقَه رو بُرد یا باخت؟ : 💬

/pe.sa.ret- mo.sǎ.be.ğa.ro- bord- yǎ- bǎǩt/

Did your son win or lose in the competition?

باخت. حالمان خیلی گرفته شد. : 🖉 ⓘ

/bǎǩt- hǎ.le.mǎn- ǩey.li- ge.ref.te- šod/

باخت. حالمون خیلی گرفته شد. : 💬 ⓘ

/bǎǩt- hǎ.le.mun- ǩey.li- ge.ref.te- šod/

He lost. We were very upset.

Disappointments

✏️ : مهمانی ات خوب برگزار شد؟
/meh.mă.ni.at- ǩub- bar.go.zǎr- šod/

💬 : مهمونیت خوب برگزار شد؟
/meh.mu.nit- ǩub- bar.go.zǎr- šod/

Did your party go well?

✏️ : نه. هیچکس نیامد.
/na- hič.kas- na.yǎ.mad/

💬 : نه. هیشکی نیومد.
/na- hiš.ki- na.yu.mad/

No. Nobody showed up.

✏️ : دیروز رفتید موزه؟
/di.ruz- raf.tid- mu.ze/

💬 : دیروز رفتین موزه؟
/di.ruz- raf.tin- mu.ze/

Did you go to the museum yesterday?

ⓘ ✏️ : رفتیم، امّا موزه بسته بود. دماغمان حسابی سوخت!
/raf.tim- am.mǎ- mu.ze- bas.te- bud- da.mǎ.ǧe.mǎn- he.sǎ.bi- suǩt/

ⓘ 💬 : رفتیم، امّا موزه بسته بود. دماغمون حسابی سوخت!
/raf.tim- am.mǎ- mu.ze- bas.te- bud- da.mǎ.ǧe.mun- he.sǎ.bi- suǩt/

We did, but the museum was closed. We were bummed out.

✏️ : مهمانی سارا خوش گذشت؟
/meh.mă.ni.ye- sǎ.rǎ- ǩoš- go.zašt/

💬 : مهمونی سارا خوش گذشت؟
/meh.mu.ni.ye- sǎ.rǎ- ǩoš- go.zašt/

Did you have a good time at Sara's party?

✏️ : بد نبود، ولی فقط من بودم وَ سینا.
/bad- na.bud- va.li- fa.ǧat- man- bu.dam- va- si.nǎ/

💬 : بد نبود، ولی فقط من بودم و سینا.
/bad- na.bud- va.li- fa.ǧat- man- bu.da.mo- si.nǎ/

It was o.k. but it was only me and Sina.

به رستوران تازه ی محلّه تان سر زدی؟ : ✎

/be- res.tu.ră.ne- tă.ze.ye- ma.hal.la.tăn- sar- za.di/

به رستوران تازه ی محلّه تون سر زدی؟ : 💬

/be- res.tu.ră.ne- tă.ze.ye- ma.hal.la.tun- sar- za.di/

Did you check out the new restaurant in your neighborhood?

آره، امّا کار و کاسبی شان خیلی کساد است. : ✎

/ă.re- am.mă- kăr- va- kă.se.bi.šăn- ḱey.li- ke.săd- ast/

آره، امّا کار و کاسبی شون خیلی کساده. : 💬

/ă.re- am.mă- kă.ro- kă.se.bi.šun- ḱey.li- ke.să.de/

Yes, but their business was very slow.

ماشینَت را از تعمیرگاه گرفتی؟ : ✎

/mă.ši.nat- ră- az- ta'.mir.găh- ge.ref.ti/

ماشینتو از تعمیرگاه گرفتی؟ : 💬

/mă.ši.ne.to- az- ta'.mir.găh- ge.ref.ti/

Did you get your car back from the repair shop?

آره. امّا سرویس شان افتضاح بود. : ✎

/ă.re- am.mă- ser.vi.se.šăn- ef.te.zăh- bud/

آره. امّا سرویس شون افتضاح بود. : 💬

/ă.re- am.mă- ser.vi.se.šun- ef.te.zăh- bud/

Yes, but their service was horrible.

از دوست من خوشَت آمد؟ : ✎

/az- dus.te- man- ḱo.šat- ă.mad/

از دوست من خوشت اومد؟ : 💬

/az- dus.te- man- ḱo.šet- u.mad/

Did you enjoy meeting my friend?

نه. اخلاقَش خیلی تندست. : ✎

/na- aḱ.lă.ğaš- ḱey.li- tond- ast/

نه. اخلاقش خیلی تنده. : 💬

/na- aḱ.lă.ğeš- ḱey.li- ton.de/

No. She has a bad temper.

کتاب تازه ات خوب فروش می رود؟ : ✏️

/ke.tă.be- tă.ze.at- ǩub- fo.ru͟ṡ- mi.ra.vad/

کتاب تازَت خوب فروش می ره؟ : 💬

/ke.tă.be- tă.zat- ǩub- fo.ru͟ṡ- mi.re/

Is your new book selling well?

نه. فروشَش کند است. : ✏️

/na- fo.ru.ṡaṡ- kond- ast/

نه. فروشش کنده. : 💬

/na- fo.ru.ṡeṡ- kon.de/

No. It is selling quite slowly.

کارتان چطورست؟ : ✏️

/kă.re.tăn- če.to.rast/

کارتون چطوره؟ : 💬

/kă.re.tun- če.to.re/

How is your business?

خوب نیست. کافی شاپ مان خیلی خلوت است. : ✏️

/ǩub- nist- kă.fi.ṡă.pe.măn- ǩeyli- ǩal.vat- ast/

خوب نیس. کافی شاپ مون خیلی خلوته. : 💬

/ǩub- nis- kă.fi.ṡă.pe.mun- ǩeyli- ǩal.va.te/

Not good. Our coffee shop has no traffic.

رستوران تان شلوغ می شود؟ : ✏️

/res.tu.ră.ne.tăn- ṡo.luǧ- mi.ṡa.vad/

رستوران تون شلوغ می شه؟ : 💬

/res.tu.ră.ne.tun- ṡo.luǧ- mi.ṡe/

Does your restaurant get crowded?

نه. به اندازه ی کافی مشتری نداریم. : 💬 ✏️

/na- be- an.dă.ze.ye- kă.fi- moṡ.ta.ri- na.dă.rim/

No. We don't have enough customers.

✐ : پسرَت کار پیدا کرد؟

/pe.sa.rat- kăr- pey.dă- kard/

💬 : پسرت کار پیدا کرد؟

/pe.sa.ret- kăr- pey.dă- kard/

Did your son find a job?

✐ : نه. هرچه می گردد، کار مناسبی پیدا نمی کند.

/na- har.če- mi.gar.dad- kă.re- mo.nă.se.bi- pey.dă- ne.mi.ko.nad/

💬 : نه. هر چی می گرده، کار مناسبی پیدا نمی کنه.

/na- har.či- mi.gar.de- kă.re- mo.nă.se.bi- pey.dă- ne.mi.ko.ne/

No. As hard as he looks, he seems to find no decent jobs.

✐ : بچّه هایت قدر زحمت هایت را می دانند؟

/bač.če.hă.yat- ğad.re- zah.mat.hă.yat- ră- mi.dă.nand/

💬 : بچّه هات قدر زحمتاتو می دونن؟

/bač.če.hăt- ğad.re- zah.ma.tă.to- mi.du.nan/

Do your children appreciate your hard work?

✐ : بهیچوجه. انگار من مستخدم شان هستم.

/be.hič.vajh- en.găr- man- mos.tak̆.te.me.šăn- has.tam/

💬 : بهیچوجه. انگار من مستخدم شونم.

/be.hič.vajh- en.găr- man- mos.tak̆.te.me.šu.nam/

Not at all; it's like I am their servant.

ⓘ ✐ : کار انتشارات تان گرفته است؟

/kă.re- en.te.šă.ră.te.tăn- ge.ref.te- ast/

ⓘ 💬 : کار انتشارات تون گرفته؟

/kă.re- en.te.šă.ră.te.tun- ge.ref.te/

Has your publishing business taken off?

ⓘ ✐ : نه. نگرفته است.

/na- na.ge.ref.te- ast/

ⓘ 💬 : نه. نگرفته.

/na- na.ge.ref.te/

No. It hasn't.

✏️ : نامزدَت کجاست؟

/năm.za.dat- ko.jăst/

💬 : نامزدت کجاس؟

/năm.za.det- ko.jăs/

Where is your fiancé ?

ⓘ ✏️ : متأسّفانه با او بهم زدم!

/mo.te.'as.se.fă.ne- bă- u- be.ham- za.dam/

ⓘ 💬 : متأسّفانه باهاش بهم زدم!

/mo.te.'as.se.fă.ne- bă.hăš- be.ham- za.dam/

Unfortunately, I broke up with him!

✏️ : عروسی تان کِی است؟

/'a.ru.si.tăn- key- ast/

💬 : عروسی تون کِیه؟

/'a.ru.si.tun- ke.ye/

When is your wedding?

ⓘ ✏️ : عروسی مان بهم خورد!

/'a.ru.si.măn- be.ham- ḱord/

ⓘ 💬 : عروسی مون بهم خورد!

/'a.ru.si.mun- be.ham- ḱord/

Our wedding is off.

✏️ : خواهرَت چطورست؟

/ḱă.ha.rat- če.to.rast/

💬 : خواهرت چطوره؟

/ḱă.ha.ret- če.to.re/

How is your sister?

✏️ : نمی دانم. ما با هم قهریم.

/ne.mi.dă.nam- mă- bă- ham- ğah.rim/

💬 : نمی دونم. ما با هم قهریم.

/ne.mi.du.nam- mă- bă- ham- ğah.rim/

I don't know. Things are sort of sour between us.

Likes

✐ : تفریح مورد علاقه ات چیست؟

/taf.ri.he- mo.re̱.de- ʼa.lă.ğe.at- čist/

💬 : تفریح مورد علاقَت چیه؟

/taf.ri.he- mo.re̱.de- ʼa.lă.ğat- či.ye/

What's your favorite hobby?

✐ : من دوست دارم نقّاشی کنم.

/man- dust- dă.ram- nağ.ğă.ši- ko.nam/

💬 : من دوس دارم نقّاشی کنم.

/man- dus- dă.ram- nağ.ğă.ši- ko.nam/

I like to paint.

✐ : دیروز در استخر دانشگاه دیدیمَت!

/di.ruz- dar- es.tak̆.re̱- dă.neš.găh- di.di.mat/

💬 : دیروز توی استخر دانشگاه دیدیمت!

/di.ruz- tu.ye- es.tak̆.re̱- dă.neš.găh- di.di.met/

We saw you at the university pool yesterday.

✐ : من از شنا کردن خوشم می آید.

/man- az- še.nă- kar.dan- k̆o.šam- mi.ă.yad/

💬 : من از شنا کردن خوشم میاد.

/man- az- še.nă- kar.dan- k̆o.šam- mi.yăd/

I like swimming.

می خواهی این تابلو را بخری؟ : ✏️

/mi.ǩǎ.hi- in- tǎb.lo- rǎ- be.ǩa.ri/

می خوای این تابلو رو بخری؟ : 💬

/mi.ǩǎy- in- tǎb.lo- ro- be.ǩa.ri/

Do you want to buy this picture?

شاید. از این نقّاشی بدم نمی آید. : ✏️

/šǎ.yad- az- in- nağ.ǧǎ.ši- ba.dam- ne.mi.ǎ.yad/

شاید. از این نقّاشی بدم نمیاد. : 💬

/šǎ.yad- az- in- nağ.ǧǎ.ši- ba.dam- ne.mi.yǎd/

Maybe. I kind of like this painting.

باز هم این هفته می خواهی بروی تئاتر؟ : ✏️

/bǎz- ham- in- haf.te- mi.ǩǎ.hi- be.ra.vi- te.'ǎtr/

بازَم این هفته می خوای بری تئاتر؟ : 💬

/bǎ.zam- in- haf.te- mi.ǩǎy- be.ri- te.'ǎtr/

Do you want to go to the theater again this week?

آره. من عاشق تئاترم. : 💬 ✏️

/ǎ.re- man- 'ǎ.še.ǧe- te.'ǎt.ram/

Yes. I love theater performances.

تنهایی به تو سخت می گُذرد؟ : ✏️

/tan.hǎ.yi- be- to- saǩt- mi.go.za.rad/

تنهایی بهت سخت می گذره؟ : 💬

/tan.hǎ.yi- be.het- saǩt- mig.za.re/

Is it hard for you to be alone?

نه. من از تنهایی اصلاً بدم نمی آید. : ✏️

/na- man- az- tan.hǎ.yi- as.lan- ba.dam- ne.mi.ǎ.yad/

نه. من از تنهایی اصلاً بدم نمیاد. : 💬

/na- man- az- tan.hǎ.yi- as.lan- ba.dam- ne.mi.yǎd/

No. I don't mind being alone.

چرا هیچوقت بیرون غذا نمی خوری؟ : ✏️ 💬

/če.ră- hič.vaǧt- bi.run- ǧa.ză- ne.mi.ǩo.ri/

Why don't you ever eat out?

چون دوست دارم خودم آشپزی کنم. : ✏️

/čon- dust- dă.ram- ǩo.dam- ăš.pa.zi- ko.nam/

چون دوس دارم خودم آشپزی کنم. : 💬

/čon- dus- dă.ram- ǩo.dam- ăš.pa.zi- ko.nam/

It's because I love to cook for myself!

دوباره امشب مهمانی داری؟ : ✏️

/do.bă.re- em.šab- meh.mă.ni- dă.ri/

دوباره امشب مهمونی داری؟ : 💬

/do.bă.re- em.šab- meh.mu.ni- dă.ri/

Are you throwing another party tonight?

آره. من اهلِ معاشرتم. : 💬 ✏️

/ă.re- man- ah.le- mo.'ă.še.ra.tam/

Yes. I like to socialize.

چرا تصمیم گرفتید فارسی بخوانید؟ : ✏️

/če.ră- tas.mim- ge.ref.tid- făr.si- be.ǩă.nid/

چرا تصمیم گرفتین فارسی بخونین؟ : 💬

/če.ră- tas.mim- ge.ref.tin- făr.si- be.ǩu.nin/

Why did you decide to learn Persian?

من ادبیات فارسی را دوست دارم. : ✏️

/man- a.da.bi.yă.te- făr.si- ră- dust- dă.ram/

من ادبیات فارسی رو دوس دارم. : 💬

/man- a.da.bi.yă.te- făr.si- ro- dus- dă.ram/

I like Persian literature.

✏️ : هنر مُدرن را دوست دارید؟

/ho.na.re- mo.dern- ră- dust- dă.rid/

💬 : هنر مُدرنو دوس دارین؟

/ho.na.re- mo.der.no- dus- dă.rin/

Do you like modern art?

✏️ : بله. هنر مدرن برای من جذّابیت خاصّی دارد.

/ba.le- ho.na.re- mo.dern- ba.ră.ye- man- jaz.ză.bi.ya.te- ǩăs.si- dă.rad/

💬 : بله. هنر مدرن برام جذّابیت خاصّی داره.

/ba.le- ho.na.re- mo.dern- ba.răm- jaz.ză.bi.ya.te- ǩăs.si- dă.re/

Yes. Modern art holds a special fascination for me.

ⓘ ✏️ : میلَت به چه می کشد؟

/mey.lat- be- če- mi.ke.šad/

ⓘ 💬 : میلت به چی می کشه؟

/mey.let- be- či- mi.ke.še/

What do you feel like eating?

✏️ : هوس بستنی کرده ام.

/ha.va.se- bas.ta.ni- kar.de.am/

💬 : هوس بستنی کردم.

/ha.va.se- bas.ta.ni- kar.dam/

I'm craving ice cream.

✏️ : این خوراک مرغ را دوست داشتی؟

/in- ǩo.ră.ke- morǧ- ră- dust- dăš.ti/

💬 : این خوراک مرغو دوس داشتی؟

/in- ǩo.ră.ke- mor.ǧo- dus- dăš.ti/

Did you like this chicken stew?

✏️ 💬 ⓘ : عالی بود. خیلی به من مزه کرد.

/'ă.li- bud- ǩey.li- be- man- ma.ze- kard/

It was great. I enjoyed it very much.

نوشیدنیِ سرد می خوری یا گرم؟ : 🖊💬

/nu.ši.da.ni.ye- sard- mi.ǩo.ri- yǎ- garm/

Would like to have a cold or a warm drink?

گرم. شیر کاکائو در این هوایِ سرد می چسبد. : 🖊ⓘ

/garm- šir.kǎ.kǎ.ʾu- dar- in- ha.vǎ.ye- sard- mi.čas.bad/

گرم. شیر کاکائو توی این هوایِ سرد می چسبه. : ⓘ💬

/garm- šir.kǎ.kǎ.ʾu- tu.ye- in- ha.vǎ.ye- sard- mi.čas.be/

Warm. Hot chocolate sounds perfect in this cold weather.

Dislikes

همیشه خودَت غذا می پزی؟ : 🖎
/ha.mi.še- ǩo.dat- ğa.zǎ- mi.pa.zi/

همیشه خودت غذا می پزی؟ : 💬
/ha.mi.še- ǩo.det- ğa.zǎ- mi.pa.zi/

Do you always cook for yourself?

بله. من دوست ندارم بیرون غذا بخورم. : 🖎
/ba.le- man- dust- na.dǎ.ram- bi.run- ğa.zǎ- be.ǩo.ram/

بله. من دوس ندارم بیرون غذا بخورم. : 💬
/ba.le- man- dus- na.dǎ.ram- bi.run- ğa.zǎ- be.ǩo.ram/

Yes. I don't like to eat out.

چرا چیزی نمی خری؟ : 🖎 💬
/če.rǎ- či.zi- ne.mi.ǩa.ri/

Why don't you buy something?

این لباس ها با سلیقه ی من جور نیستند. : 🖎
/in- le.bǎs.hǎ- bǎ- sa.li.ğe.ye- man- jur- nis.tand/

این لباسا با سلیقَم جور نیستن. : 💬
/in- le.bǎ.sǎ- bǎ- sa.li.ğam- jur- nis.tan/

These clothes are not quite my taste.

چرا دیشب با ما نیامدی؟ : ✏️

/če.rǎ- di.šab- bǎ- mǎ- na.yǎ.ma.di/

چرا دیشب با ما نیومدی؟ : 💬

/če.rǎ- di.šab- bǎ- mǎ- na.yu.ma.di/

Why didn't you come with us last night?

از دوست هایت خوشم نمی آید. : ✏️

/az- dust.hǎ.yat- ǩo.šam- ne.mi.ǎ.yad/

از دوستات خوشم نمیاد. : 💬

/az- dus.tǎt- ǩo.šam- ne.mi.yǎd/

I don't like your friends.

در مهمانی سارا ندیدمَت! : ✏️

/dar- meh.mǎ.ni.ye- sǎ.rǎ- na.di.da.mat/

توی مهمونی سارا ندیدمت! : 💬

/tu.ye- meh.mu.ni.ye- sǎ.rǎ- na.di.da.met/

I didn't see you at Sara's party.

من اهل مهمانی رفتن نیستم. : ✏️

/man- ah.le- meh.mǎ.ni- raf.tan- nis.tam/

من اهل مهمونی رفتن نیستم. : 💬

/man- ah.le- meh.mu.ni- raf.tan- nis.tam/

I'm not the party going type.

چرا آپارتمانَت را در شهر فروختی؟ : ✏️

/če.rǎ- ǎ.pǎr.te.mǎ.nat- rǎ- dar- šahr- fo.ruǩ.ti/

چرا آپارتمانتو توی شهر فروختی؟ : 💬

/če.rǎ- ǎ.pǎr.te.mǎ.ne.to- tu.ye- šahr- fo.ruǩ.ti/

Why did you sell your apartment in the city?

من اصلاً تحمّل ترافیک شهر را ندارم. : ✏️

/man- as.lan- ta.ham.mo.le- te.rǎ.fi.ke- šahr- rǎ- na.dǎ.ram/

من اصلاً تحمّل ترافیک شهرو ندارم. : 💬

/man- as.lan- ta.ham.mo.le- te.rǎ.fi.ke- šah.ro- na.dǎ.ram/

I can't stand the city's traffic.

هفته ی گذشته با دوستانَت نرفتی کنسرت؟ : ✏

/haf.te.ye- go.zaš.te- bă- dus.tă.nat- na.raf.ti- kon.sert/

هفته ی پیش با دوستات نرفتی کنسرت؟ : 💬

/haf.te.ye- piš- bă- dus.tăt- na.raf.ti- kon.sert/

Didn't you go to a concert with your friends last week?

نه. موزیک بلند اعصابم را بهم می ریزد. : ✏ ⓘ

/na- mu.zi.ke- bo.land- aʼ.să.bam- ră- be.ham- mi.ri.zad/

نه. موزیک بلند اعصابمو می ریزه بهم. : 💬 ⓘ

/na- mu.zi.ke- bo.land- aʼ.să.ba.mo- mi.ri.ze- be.ham/

No. Loud music gets on my nerves.

چرا هروقت بحث سیاسی می شود تو ساکت می مانی؟ : ✏

/če.ră- har- vağt- bah.se- si.yă.si- mi.ša.vad- to- să.ket- mi.mă.ni/

چرا هروقت بحث سیاسی می شه تو ساکت می مونی؟ : 💬

/če.ră- har- vağt- bah.se- si.yă.si- mi.še- to- să.ket- mi.mu.ni/

Why do you stay quiet whenever there is a political discussion?

سیاست حالَم را بهم می زند. : ✏

/si.yă.sat- hă.lam- ră- be.ham- mi.za.nad/

سیاست حالَمو بهم می زنه. : 💬

/si.yă.sat- hă.la.mo- be.ham- mi.za.ne/

Politics make me sick.

به غذایَت لب نزدی! : ✏ ⓘ

/be- ğa.ză.yat- lab- na.za.di/

به غذات لب نزدی! : 💬 ⓘ

/be- ğa.zăt- lab- na.za.di/

You didn't touch your food!

زیاد طرفدار غذاهای تند نیستم. : 💬 ✏

/zi.yăd- ta.raf.dă.re- ğa.ză.hă.ye- tond- nis.tam/

I'm not a fan of spicy food.

چرا تابستان نمی روی یک جایی؟ : ✏

/če.rǎ- tǎ.bes.tǎn- ne.mi.ra.vi- yek- jǎ.yi/

چرا تابستون نمی ری یه جایی؟ : 💬

/če.rǎ- tǎ.bes.tun- ne.mi.ri- ye- jǎ.yi/

Why don't you go somewhere in the summer?

از سفر متنفّرم. : 💬 ✏

/az- sa.far- mo.te.naf.fe.ram/

I hate traveling.

چرا دیگر با سینا رفت وَ آمد نمی کنی؟ : ✏

/če.rǎ- di.gar- bǎ- si.nǎ- raft- va- ǎ.mad- ne.mi.ko.ni/

چرا دیگه با سینا رفت و آمد نمی کنی؟ : 💬

/če.rǎ- di.ge- bǎ- si.nǎ- raf.to- ǎ.mad- ne.mi.ko.ni/

Why did you stop hanging out with Sina?

از رفتارَش بدم می آید. : ✏

/az- raf.tǎ.raš- ba.dam- mi.ǎ.yad/

از رفتارِش بدم میاد. : 💬

/az- raf.tǎ.reš- ba.dam- mi.yǎd/

I don't like the way he behaves.

Preferences & Comparisons

✏️ : بسکتبال را بیشتر دوست داری یا فوتبال را؟

/bas.ket.băl- ră- biš.tar- dust- dă.ri- yă- fut.băl- ră/

💬 : بسکتبالو بیشتر دوس داری یا فوتبالو؟

/bas.ket.bă.lo- biš.tar- dus- dă.ri- yă- fut.bă.lo/

Which do you like better: basketball or soccer?

✏️ : من از بسکتبال بیشتر از فوتبال خوشم می آید.

/man- az- bas.ket.băl- biš.tar- az- fut.băl- ǩo.šam- mi.ă.yad/

💬 : من از بسکتبال بیشتر از فوتبال خوشم میاد.

/man- az- bas.ket.băl- biš.tar- az- fut.băl- ǩo.šam- mi.yăd/

I like basketball better than soccer.

✏️ : غذای چینی از همه ی غذاها خوشمزه ترست!

/ǧa.ză.ye- či.ni- az- ha.me.ye- ǧa.ză.hă- ǩoš.ma.ze.ta.rast/

💬 : غذای چینی از همه ی غذاها خوشمزه تره!

/ǧa.ză.ye- či.ni- az- ha.me.ye- ǧa.ză.hă- ǩoš.ma.ze.ta.re/

Chinese food is more delicious than any other type of food!

✏️ : من غذای ایتالیایی را به غذای چینی ترجیح می دهم.

/man- ǧa.ză.ye- i.tă.li.yă.yi- ră- be- ǧa.ză.ye- či.ni- tar.jih- mi.da.ham/

💬 : من غذای ایتالیایی رو به غذای چینی ترجیح می دم.

/man- ǧa.ză.ye- i.tă.li.yă.yi- ro- be- ǧa.ză.ye- či.ni- tar.jih- mi.dam/

I prefer Italian food to Chinese food.

چرا با سارا مشورت نکردی؟ : ✏️ 💬

/če.ră- bă- să.ră- maš.ve.rat- na.kar.di/

Why didn't you consult with Sara?

من آنقدر که به تو نزدیکم، به سارا نزدیک نیستم. : ✏️

/man- ăn.ğadr- ke- be- to- naz.di.kam- be- să.ră- naz.dik- nis.tam/

من اونقدر که به تو نزدیکم، به سارا نزدیک نیستم. : 💬

/man- un.ğadr- ke- be- to- naz.di.kam- be- să.ră- naz.dik- nis.tam/

I am not as close to Sara as I am to you.

موضوع را به خواهرَت هَم گفتی؟ : ✏️

/mo.zu'- ră- be- kă.ha.rat- ham- gof.ti/

موضوع رو به خواهرِتَم گفتی؟ : 💬

/mo.zu'- ro- be- kă.ha.re.tam- gof.ti/

Did you also tell the story to your sister?

نه. ترجیح می دهم با تو حرف بزنم تا با خواهرم. : ✏️

/na- tar.jih- mi.da.ham- bă- to- harf- be.za.nam- tă- bă- kă.ha.ram/

نه. ترجیح می دم با تو حرف بزنم تا با خواهرم. : 💬

/na- tar.jih- mi.dam- bă- to- harf- be.za.nam- tă- bă- kă.ha.ram/

No. I prefer talking to you rather than talking to my sister.

قرارست فردا برف بیاید. : ✏️

/ğa.ră.rast- far.dă- barf- bi.yă.yad/

قراره فردا برف بیاد. : 💬

/ğa.ră.re- far.dă- barf- bi.yăd/

It's supposed to snow tomorrow.

برف بیاید یا نیاید برای من فرقی نمی کند. : ✏️

/barf- bi.yă.yad- yă- na.yă.yad- bā.ră.ye- man- far.ği- ne.mi.ko.nad/

برف بیاد یا نیاد برای من فرقی نمی کنه. : 💬

/barf- bi.yăd- yă- na.yăd- ba.ră.ye- man- far.ği- ne.mi.ko.ne/

It's all the same to me whether it snows or not.

خانه ی تو بزرگ ترست یا خانه ی سینا؟ : ✎

/kǎ.ne.ye- to- bo.zorg.ta.rast- yǎ- kǎ.ne.ye- si.nǎ/

خونه ی تو بزرگ تره یا خونه ی سینا؟ : 💬

/ku.ne.ye- to- bo.zorg.ta.re- yǎ- ku.ne.ye- si.nǎ/

Which one is bigger: your house or Sina's house?

خانه ی من از خانه ی سینا خیلی بزرگ ترست! : ✎

/kǎ.ne.ye- man- az- kǎ.ne.ye- si.nǎ- key.li- bo.zorg.ta.rast/

خونه ی من از خونه ی سینا خیلی بزرگتره! : 💬

/ku.ne.ye- man- az- ku.ne.ye- si.nǎ- key.li- bo.zorg.ta.re/

My house is much bigger than Sina's.

بنظر تو یادگیری زبان فارسی ساده ترست یا زبان عربی؟ : ✎

/be.na.za.re- to- yǎd.gi.ri.ye- za.bǎ.ne- fǎr.si- sǎ.de.ta.rast- yǎ- za.bǎ.ne- 'a.ra.bi/

بنظر تو یاد گرفتن زبون فارسی ساده تره یا زبون عربی؟ : 💬

/be.na.za.re- to- yǎd- ge.ref.ta.ne- za.bu.ne- fǎr.si- sǎ.de.ta.re- yǎ- za.bu.ne- 'a.ra.bi/

Which language you think is easier to learn: Persian or Arabic?

فکر می کنم از نظر سختی هر دوشان مثل هم باشند. : ✎

/fekr- mi.ko.nam- az- na.za.re- sak.ti- har- do.šǎn- mes.le- ham- bǎ.šand/

فکر می کنم از نظر سختی هر دوشون مثل هم باشن. : 💬

/fekr- mi.ko.nam- az- na.za.re- sak.ti- har- do.šun- mes.le- ham- bǎ.šan/

I think they are equally difficult to learn.

لیلا خیلی خوشگل است! : ✎

/ley.lǎ- key.li- koš.gel- ast/

لیلا خیلی خوشگله! : 💬

/ley.lǎ- key.li- koš.ge.le/

Leila is so beautiful!

بله. لیلا از تمام خواهرهایش خوشگل ترست! : ✎

/ba.le- ley.lǎ- az- ta.mǎ.me- kǎ.har.hǎ.yaš- koš.gel.ta.rast/

آره. لیلا از همه ی خواهرهاش خوشگل تره! : 💬

/ǎ.re- ley.lǎ- az- ha.me.ye- kǎ.har.hǎš- koš.gel.ta.re/

Yes. Leila is more beautiful than all her sisters!

✎ : استادتان چطورست؟

/os.tǎ.de.tǎn- če.to.rast/

💬 : استادتون چطوره؟

/os.tǎ.de.tun- če.to.re/

How is your professor?

✎ : استادمان بهترین استاد فارسیِ این دانشگاه است.

/os.tǎ.de.mǎn- beh.ta.rin- os.tǎ.de- fǎr.si.ye- in- dǎ.neš.gǎh- ast/

💬 : استادمون بهترین استاد فارسیِ این دانشگاس.

/os.tǎ.de.mun- beh.ta.rin- os.tǎ.de- fǎr.si.ye- in- dǎ.neš.gǎs./

Our professor is the best Persian instructor of this university.

✎ : از شیکاگو خوشَت آمد؟

/az- ši.kǎ.go- ǩo.šat- ǎ.mad/

💬 : از شیکاگو خوشَت اومد؟

/az- ši.kǎ.go- ǩo.šet- u.mad/

Did you like Chicago?

✎ : بله، امّا هیچ کجا به قشنگیِ لوس آنجلس نیست.

/ba.le- am.mǎ- hič- ko.jǎ- be- ǧa.šan.gi.ye- los- ǎn.ge.les- nist/

💬 : آره، امّا هیچ جا به قشنگیِ لوس آنجلس نیس.

/ǎ.re- am.mǎ- hič- jǎ- be- ǧa.šan.gi.ye- los- ǎn.ge.les- nis/

Yes, but there is no place as beautiful as Los Angeles.

Feelings

حالَت چطورست؟ : ✏️

/hă.lat- če.to.rast/

حالت چطوره؟ : 💬

/hă.let- če.to.re/

How are you doing?

خیلی هیجانزده ام! : ✏️

/ǩey.li- ha.ye.jăn.za.de.am/

خیلی هیجانزدَم! : 💬

/ǩey.li- ha.ye.jăn.za.dam/

I'm so excited!

حالَت خوب است؟ : ✏️

/hă.lat- ǩub- ast/

حالت خوبه! : 💬

/hă.let- ǩu.be/

Are you o.k.?

آره. خیلی سرحالم. : 💬 ✏️

/ă.re- ǩey.li- sar.hă.lam/

Yes. I'm in a really good mood.

✏️ : چه ات است؟

/če.at- ast/

💬 : چته؟

/če.te/

What's the matter with you?

✏️ : خیلی خیلی عصبانی هستم.

/ǩey.li- ǩey.li- 'a.sa.bǎ.ni- has.tam/

💬 : خیلی خیلی عصبانیَم.

/ǩey.li- ǩey.li- 'a.sa.bǎ.ni.yam/

I'm extremely angry.

✏️💬 : چرا اینقدر ساکتی؟

/če.rǎ- in.ğadr- sǎ.ke.ti/

Why are you so quiet?

✏️ : احساس افسردگی می کنم.

/eh.sǎ.se- af.sor.de.gi- mi.ko.nam/

💬 : احساس می کنم افسردَم.

/eh.sǎs- mi.ko.nam- af.sor.dam/

I feel depressed.

✏️ : اتّفاقی افتاده است؟

/et.te.fǎ.ği- of.tǎ.de- ast/

💬 : اتّفاقی افتاده؟

/et.te.fǎ.ği- of.tǎ.de/

Has something happened?

✏️ : نه. امّا یک کم نگرانم.

/na- am.mǎ- yek- kam- ne.ga.rǎ.nam/

💬 : نه. امّا یه کم نگرانم.

/na- am.mǎ- ye- kam- ne.ga.rǎ.nam/

No, but I am a bit worried.

✏️ : چه شده است؟

/če- šo.de- ast/

💬 : چی شده؟

/či- šo.de/

What's wrong?

✏️ : چیزی نشده است. فقط خسته ام.

/či.zi- na.šo.de- ast- fa.ğat- ǩas.te.am/

💬 : چیزی نشده. فقط خستَم.

/či.zi- na.šo.de- fa.ğat- ǩas.tam/

Nothing. I'm just tired.

💬 ⓘ : توی خودتی!

/tu.ye- ǩo.de.ti/

You seem preoccupied!

✏️ ⓘ : چیزی نیست. حوصله ام سر رفته است.

/či.zi- nist- ho.se.le.am- sar- raf.te- ast/

💬 ⓘ : چیزی نیس. حوصلَم سر رفته.

/či.zi- nis- ho.se.lam- sar- raf.te/

It's nothing. I'm bored.

✏️ : موضوع چیست؟

/mo.zu'- čist/

💬 : موضوع چیه؟

/mo.zu'- či.ye/

What's going on?

✏️ : اعصابم ناراحت است!

/a'.să.bam- nă.ră.hat- ast/

💬 : اعصابم ناراحته!

/a'.să.bam- nă.ră.ha.te/

I'm a bundle of nerves right now!

✎ : همه چیز خوب است؟

/ha.me- čiz- ǩub- ast/

💬 : همه چی خوبه؟

/ha.me- či- ǩu.be/

Is everything o.k.?

✎ : آره. روحیه ام خیلی عالی است.

/ǎ.re- ru.hi.ye.am- ǩey.li- 'ǎ.li- ast/

💬 : آره. روحیَم خیلی عالیه.

/ǎ.re- ru.hi.yam- ǩey.li- 'ǎ.li.ye/

Yes. I'm in really good spirits.

ⓘ ✎ : چشم هایَت برق می زنند!

/čašm.hǎ.yat- barǧ- mi.za.nand/

ⓘ 💬 : چشمات برق می زنن!

/čašm.hǎt- barǧ- mi.za.nan/

Your eyes are sparkling!

ⓘ ✎ : از خوشحالی توی پوستم نمی گنجم.

/az- ǩoš.hǎ.li- tu.ye- pus.tam- ne.mi.gon.jam/

I'm jumping for joy.

Personality Traits & Characteristics

باز هم کلیدَت را گم کرده ای؟ : ✏️

/bǎz- ham- ke.li.dat- rǎ- gom- kar.de.i/

بازَم کلیدِتو گم کردی؟ : 💬

/bǎ.zam- ke.li.de.to- gom- kar.di/

Have you lost your key again?

آره. من اصولاً آدمِ حواس پرتی هستم. : ✏️

/ǎ.re- man- o.su.lan- ǎ.da.me- ha.vǎs.par.ti- has.tam/

آره. من اصولاً آدمِ حواس پرتیَم. : 💬

/ǎ.re- man- o.su.lan- ǎ.da.me- ha.vǎs.par.ti.yam/

Yes. I'm generally a forgetful person.

چرا خواهرَت زیاد حرف نمی زند؟ : ✏️

/če.rǎ- kǎ.ha.rat- zi.yǎd- harf- ne.mi.za.nad/

چرا خواهرت زیاد حرف نمی زنه؟ : 💬

/če.rǎ- kǎ.ha.ret- zi.yǎd- harf- ne.mi.za.ne/

Why doesn't your sister talk much?

خیلی خجالتی است. : ✏️

/ǩey.li- ǩe.jǎ.la.tist/

خیلی خجالتیه. : 💬

/ǩey.li- ǩe.jǎ.la.ti.ye/

She is very shy.

من اصلاً از همکارَت خوشم نیامد. : ✏️

/man- as.lan- az- ham.kǎ.rat- ǩo.šam- na.yǎ.mad/

من اصلاً از همکارت خوشم نیومد. : 💬

/man- as.lan- az- ham.kǎ.ret- ǩo.šam- na.yu.mad/

I didn't like your coworker at all.

می دانم. خیلی بی اَدب است. : ✏️

/mi.dǎ.nam- ǩey.li- bi.a.dab- ast/

می دونم. خیلی بی اَدبه. : 💬

/mi.du.nam- ǩey.li- bi.a.da.be/

I know. He is very rude.

همه رئیس تازه را دوست دارند! : ✏️

/ha.me- ra.'i.se- tǎ.ze- rǎ- dust- dǎ.rand/

همه رئیس تازه رو دوس دارن! : 💬

/ha.me- ra.'i.se- tǎ.za.ro- dus- dǎ.ran/

Everybody loves the new boss!

علّتَش این است که خیلی خاکی است. : ✏️

/'el.la.taš- in- ast- ke- ǩey.li- ǩǎ.ki- ast/

علّتش اینه که خیلی خاکیه. : 💬

/'el.la.teš- i.ne- ke- ǩey.li- ǩǎ.ki.ye/

It's because he is very down to earth.

لطفاً دیر نکنید! : ✏️

/lot.fan- dir- na.ko.nid/

لطفاً دیر نکنین! : 💬

/lot.fan- dir- na.ko.nin/

Please don't be late!

نه نمی کنم. من آدمِ وقت شناسی هستم. : ✏️

/na- ne.mi.ko.nam- man- ǎ.da.me- vaǧt.še.nǎ.si- has.tam/

نه نمی کنم. من آدمِ وقت شناسیَم. : 💬

/na- ne.mi.ko.nam- man- ǎ.da.me- vaǧt.še.nǎ.si.yam/

I won't. I'm a very punctual person.

✎ : حرف لیلا را باور می کنی؟

/har.fe- ley.lă- ră- bă.var- mi.ko.ni/

💬 : حرف لیلا رو باور می کنی؟

/har.fe- ley.lă- ro- bă.var- mi.ko.ni/

Do you believe Leila?

✎ آره. لیلا دروغگو نیست.

/ă.re- ley.lă- do.ruğ.gu- nist/

💬 آره. لیلا دروغگو نیس.

/ă.re- ley.lă- do.ruğ.gu- nis/

Yes, I do. Leila is not a liar.

✎ : گارسون کیف پولم را پیدا کرد وَ به من پس داد.

/găr.son- ki.fe- pu.lam- ră- pey.dă- kard- va- be- man- pas- dăd/

💬 : گارسون کیف پولمو پیدا کرد و بهم پس داد.

/găr.son- ki.fe- pu.la.mo- pey.dă- kar.do- be.hem- pas- dăd/

The waiter found my wallet and returned it to me.

✎ : باید آدم درستکاری باشد.

/bă.yad- ă.da.me- do.rost.kă.ri- bă.šad/

💬 : باید آدم درستکاری باشه.

/bă.yad- ă.da.me- do.rost.kă.ri- bă.še/

He must be a decent person.

✎ : این رئیس تازه جوابِ سلام من را نمی دهد.

/in- ra.'i.se- tă.ze- ja.vă.be- sa.lă.me- man- ră- ne.mi.da.had/

💬 : این رئیس تازه جوابِ سلامَمو نمی ده.

/in- ra.'i.se- tă.ze- ja.vă.be- sa.lă.ma.mo- ne.mi.de/

This new boss doesn't return my greeting.

✎ : آره. خیلی از خود راضی است.

/ă.re- ǩey.li- az.ǩod.ră.zi- ast/

💬 : آره. خیلی از خود راضیه.

/ă.re- ǩey.li- az.ǩod.ră.zi.ye/

Yes. He is very obnoxious.

✎ : نمی دانم چرا سینا اینقدر رفتارَش با من سردست.

/ne.mi.dă.nam- če.ră- si.nă- in.ğadr- raf.tă.raš- bă- man- sar.dast/

💬 : نمی دونم چرا سینا اینقدر رفتارش با من سرده.

/ne.mi.du.nam- če.ră- si.nă- in.ğadr- raf.tă.reš- bă- man- sar.de/

I don't know why Sina is acting so cold toward me.

✎ : به تو حسودی می کند.

/be- to- ha.su.di- mi.ko.nad/

💬 : بهت حسودی می کنه.

/be.het- ha.su.di- mi.ko.ne/

He is jealous of you.

✎ : سارا برایَم سوپ درست کرده است!

/să.ră- ba.ră.yam- sup- do.rost- kar.de- ast/

💬 : سارا برام سوپ درست کرده!

/să.ră- ba.răm- sup- do.rost- kar.de/

Sara made soup for me!

✎ : دختر خیلی مهربانی است.

/dok.ta.re- key.li- meh.ra.bă.ni- ast/

💬 : خیلی دختر مهربونیه.

/key.li- dok.ta.re- meh.ra.bu.ni.ye/

She is a very kind girl.

✎ : چرا دیگر با سینا حرف نمی زنی؟

/če.ră- di.gar- bă- si.nă- harf- ne.mi.za.ni/

💬 : چرا دیگه با سینا حرف نمی زنی؟

/če.ră- di.ge- bă- si.nă- harf- ne.mi.za.ni/

Why don't you talk to Sina anymore?

✎ : سینا آدم بددهنی است.

/si.nă- ă.da.e- bad.da.ha.ni- ast/

💬 : سینا آدم بددهنیه.

/si.nă- ă.da.me- bad.da.ha.ni.ye/

He is a foul-mouthed type of person.

✎ 🗨 : چرا اینقدر از زندگی لیلا می پرسی؟

/če.rǎ- in.ǧadr- az- zen.de.gi ye- ley.lǎ- mi.por.si/

Why do you ask so much about Leila's life?

✎ : دلیل خاصّی ندارد. فقط کنجکاوم.

/da.li.le- ǩǎs.si- na.dǎ.rad- fa.ǧat- konj.kǎ.vam/

🗨 : دلیل خاصّی نداره. فقط کنجکاوم.

/da.li.le- ǩǎs.si- na.dǎ.re- fa.ǧat- konj.kǎ.vam/

No special reason. I'm just curious.

✎ : نمی فهمم چرا سام اینقدر از لیلا می پرسد!

/ne.mi.fah.mam- če.rǎ- sǎm- in.ǧadr- az- ley.lǎ- mi.por.sad/

🗨 : نمی فهمم چرا سام اینقدر از لیلا می پرسه!

/ne.mi.fah.mam- če.rǎ- sǎm- in.ǧadr- az- ley.lǎ- mi.por.se/

I don't understand why Sam asks so much about Leila!

✎ : سام به طور کلّی آدم فضولی ست.

/sǎm- be- to.re- kol.li- ǎ.da.me- fo.zu.list/

🗨 : سام به طور کلّی آدم فضولیه.

/sǎm- be- to.re- kol.li- ǎ.da.me- fo.zu.li.ye/

Sam is a nosy person.

✎ : می توانم به خواهرَت اعتماد کنم؟

/mi.ta.vǎ.nam- be- ǩǎ.ha.rat- e'.te.mǎd- ko.nam/

🗨 : می توونم به خواهرت اعتماد کنم؟

/mi.tu.nam- be- ǩǎ.ha.rat- e'.te.mǎd- ko.nam/

Can I trust your sister?

✎ : آره. خواهرم آدم بسیار بامسئولیتی است.

/ǎ.re- ǩǎ.ha.ram- ǎ.da.me- bes.yǎr- bǎ.mas.'u.li.ya.ti- ast/

🗨 : آره. خواهرم خیلی آدم بامسئولیتیه.

/ǎ.re- ǩǎ.ha.ram- ǩey.li- ǎ.da.me- bǎ.mas.'u.li.ya.ti.ye/

Yes. My sister is a very responsible person.

Farewells

✏ : خداحافظ!

/ǩo.dǎ.hǎ.fez/

💬 : خدافظ!

/ǩo.dǎ.fez/

Good bye!

✏ : فعلاً خداحافظ!

/fe'.lan- ǩo.dǎ.hǎ.fez/

💬 : فعلاً خدافظ!

/fe'.lan- ǩo.dǎ.fez/

Good bye for now!

✏ : خدا نگهدار، سفرتان بخیر!

/ǩo.dǎ.ne.gah.dǎr- sa.fa.re.tǎn- be.ǩeyr/

💬 : خدا نگهدار، سفرتون بخیر!

/ǩo.dǎ.ne.gah.dǎr- sa.fa.re.tun- be.ǩeyr/

Good bye and have a nice trip!

💬 ✏ : سفر شما هم بخیر!

/sa.fa.re- šo.mǎ- ham- be.ǩeyr/

You have a nice trip too!

به امید دیدار! : 🖉 💬

/be- omi.de- di.dăr/

Hope to see you again!

به امید دیدار نزدیک! : 🖉 💬

/be- o.mi.de- di.dă.re- naz.dik/

Hope to see you soon!

از آشنایی تان خوشوقت شدم. : 🖉

/az- ăš.nă.yi.tăn- ǩoš.vaǧt- šo.dam/

از آشنایی تون خوشوقت شدم. : 💬

/az- ăš.nă.yi.tun- ǩoš.vaǧt- šo.dam/

It was nice meeting you.

من هم همینطور. : 🖉 💬

/man- ham- ha.min.tor/

You too.

از دیدن تان خیلی خوشحال شدم. : 🖉

/az- di.da.ne.tăn- ǩey.li- ǩoš.hăl- šo.dam/

از دیدن تون خیلی خوشحال شدم. : 💬

/az- di.da.ne.tun- ǩey.li- ǩoš.hăl- šo.dam/

It was great to see you.

من هم خیلی خوشحال شدم. : 🖉

/man- ham- ǩey.li- ǩoš.hăl- šo.dam/

منَم خیلی خوشحال شدم. : 💬

/ma.nam- ǩey.li- ǩoš.hăl- šo.dam/

It was great to see you too.

✏️ 👔 : از مصاحبتِ تان لذّت بردم.

/az- mo.sǎ.he.ba.te.tǎn- lez.zat- bor.dam/

💬 👔 : از مصاحبتِ تون لذّت بردم.

/az- mo.sǎ.he.ba.te.tun- lez.zat- bor.dam/

I enjoyed talking to you.

✏️ 💬 👔 : به همچنین.

/be- ham.če.nin/

Likewise.

✏️ : باز هم به ما سر بزن.

/bǎz- ham- be- mǎ- sar- be.zan/

💬 : بازَم به ما سر بزن.

/bǎ.zam- be- mǎ- sar- be.zan/

Drop in sometime.

✏️ 💬 : حتماً !

/hat.man/

Sure!

✏️ 💬 : با هم در تماس باشیم.

/bǎ- ham- dar- ta.mǎs- bǎ.šim/

We should keep in touch.

✏️ 💬 : صد در صد.

/sad- dar- sad/

Sure thing.

باید دوباره دور هم جمع بشویم. : 🖉

/bǎ.yad- do.bǎ.re- do.re- ham- jamʿ- be.ša.vim/

باید دوباره دور هم جمع بشیم. : 💬

/bǎ.yad- do.bǎ.re- do.re- ham- jamʿ- be.šim/

We should get together again.

حتماً این کار را می کنیم! : 🖉

/hat.man- in- kǎr- rǎ- mi.ko.nim/

حتماً این کارو می کنیم! : 💬

/hat.man- in- kǎ.ro- mi.ko.nim/

We surely will.

باز هم پیش ما بیایید. : 🖉

/bǎz- ham- pi.še- mǎ- bi.yǎ.yid/

بازَم پیش ما بیاین. : 💬

/bǎ.zam- pi.še- mǎ- bi.yǎyn/

Come and visit us again.

چَشم، در اوّلین فرصت! : 🖉 💬 🗣

/čašm- dar- av.va.lin- for.sat/

Sure, the first chance I get!

برای شما آرزوی موفّقیت می کنم! : 🖉

/ba.rǎ.ye- šo.mǎ- ǎ.re.zu.ye- mo.vaf.fa.ği.yat- mi.ko.nam/

براتون آرزوی موفّقیت می کنم! : 💬

/ba.rǎ.tun- ǎ.re.zu.ye- mo.vaf.fa.ği.yat- mi.ko.nam/

I wish you all the best!

مرسی. شما هم موفّق باشید! : 🖉

/mer.si- šo.mǎ- ham- mo.vaf.fağ- bǎ.šid/

Thank you. The same to you!

✏️ : مواظبِ خودتان باشید.

/mo.vă.ze.be- ǩo.de.tăn- bă.šid/

💬 : مواظبِ خودتون باشین.

/mo.vă.ze.be- ǩo.de.tun- bă.šin/

Take care of yourself.

✏️ 💬 : ممنونم. شما هم همینطور.

/mam.nu.nam- šo.mă- ham- ha.min.tor/

Thank you. You do the same.

Courtesy

✏ : می توانم با سارا صحبت کنم؟

/mi.ta.vă.nam- bă- să.ră- soh.bat- ko.nam/

💬 : می توونم با سارا صحبت کنم؟

/mi.tu.nam- bă- să.ră- soh.bat- ko.nam/

May I speak with Sara?

✏ : سارا خانه نیست. لطفاً بعداً تماس بگیرید.

/să.ră- kă.ne- nist- lot.fan- ba'.dan- ta.măs- be.gi.rid/

💬 : سارا خونه نیس. لطفاً بعداً تماس بگیرین.

/să.ră- ku.ne- nis- lot.fan- ba'.dan- ta.măs- be.gi.rin/

Sara is not home. Please call later.

✏ : می شود لطفاً پنجره را باز کنید؟

/mi.ša.vad- lot.fan- pan.je.re- ră- băz- ko.nid/

💬 : می شه لطفاً پنجره رو باز کنین؟

/mi.še- lot.fan- pan.je.ra.ro- băz- ko.nin/

Would you please open the window?

💬✏ : همین الآن باز می کنم.

/ha.min- al.ăn- băz- mi.ko.nam/

I will open it right away.

عذر می خواهم، می شود به من کمک کنید موزه را پیدا کنم؟ : ✐

/'ozr- mi. k̆ă.ham- mi.ša.vad- be- man- ko.mak- ko.nid- mu.ze- ră- pey.dă- ko.nam/

عذر می خوام، می شه به من کمک کنین موزه رو پیدا کنم؟ : 💬

/'ozr- mi.k̆ăm- mi.še- be- man- ko.mak- ko.nin- mu.za.ro- pey.dă- ko.nam/

Excuse me. Would you please help me find the museum?

حتماً. موزه سر خیابان اصلی است. : ✐

/hat.man- mu.ze- sa.re- k̆i.yă.bă.ne- as.list/

حتماً. موزه سر خیابون اصلیه. : 💬

/hat.man- mu.ze- sa.re- k̆i.yă.bu.ne- as.li.ye/

Sure. The museum is at the corner of the main street.

چه کار می توانم برایتان بکنم؟ : ✐

/če- kăr- mi.ta.vă.nam- ba.ră.ye.tăn- be.ko.nam/

چه کار می توونم براتون بکنم؟ : 💬

/če- kăr- mi.tu.nam- ba.ră.tun- be.ko.nam/

What can I do for you?

ممنون می شوم اگر پیغام من را به سارا برسانید. : ✐

/mam.nun- mi.ša.vam- a.gar- pey.ğă.me- man- ră- be- să.ră- be.re.să.nid/

ممنون می شم اگه پیغام منو به سارا برسونین. : 💬

/mam.nun- mi.šam- a.ge- pey.ğă.me- ma.no- be- să.ră- be.re.su.nin/

I would be grateful if you would pass my message along to Sara.

ببخشید کسی اینجا می نشیند؟ : ✐

/be.bak̆.šid- ka.si- in.jă- mi.ne.ši.nad/

ببخشید کسی اینجا می شینه؟ : 💬

/be.bak̆.šid- ka.si- in.jă- mi.ši.ne/

Excuse me. Is anyone sitting here?

بله. من جای کسی را برایش نگه داشته ام. : ✐

/ba.le- man- jă.ye- ka.si- ră- ba.ră.yaš- ne.gah- dăš.te.am/

بله. من جای کسی رو براش نگه داشتم. : 💬

/ba.le- man- jă.ye- ka.si- ro- ba.răš- ne.gah- dăš.tam/

Yes. I'm holding it for someone.

✎ : ببخشید، این صندلی مال کسی است؟

/be.baǩ.šid- in- san.da.li- mǎ.le- ka.si- ast/

💬 : ببخشید، این صندلی مال کسیه؟

/be.baǩ.šid- in- san.da.li- mǎ.le- ka.si.ye/

Excuse me. Is this chair taken?

✎ : نه. می توانید آن را بردارید.

/na- mi.ta.vǎ.nid- ǎn- rǎ- bar.dǎ.rid/

💬 : نه. می توونین برش دارین.

/na- mi.tu.nin- ba.reš- dǎ.rin/

No. You can take it.

ⓘ ✎ : کمکی از دستِ من برمی آید؟

/ko.ma.ki- az- das.te- man- bar.mi.ǎ.yad/

ⓘ 💬 : کمکی از دستِ من برمیاد؟

/ko.ma.ki- az- das.te- man- bar.mi.yǎd/

Can I help you in any way?

✎ : اگر زحمت نیست، لطفاً این مقاله را یک بارِ دیگر مرور کنید.

/a.gar- zah.mat- nist- lot.fan- in- ma.ğǎ.le- rǎ- yek- bǎ.re- di.gar- mo.rur- ko.nid/

💬 : اگه زحمت نیس، لطفاً این مقاله رو یه بارِ دیگه مرور کنین.

/a.ge- zah.mat- nis- lot.fan- in- ma.ğǎ.la.ro- ye- bǎ.re- di.ge- mo.rur- ko.nin/

If it's not too much trouble, please go through this article one more time.

✎ : از کمک تان متشکّرم.

/az- ko.ma.ke.tǎn- mo.te.šak.ke.ram/

💬 : از کمک تون متشکّرم.

/az- ko.ma.ke.tun- mot.šak.ke.ram/

Thanks for your help.

💬 ✎ : خواهش می کنم.

/ǩǎ.heš- mi.ko.nam/

You are welcome.

نمی دانم با چه زبانی از شما تشکّر کنم. : ✏️ 🎩

/ne.mi.dă.nam- bă- če- za.bă.ni- az- šo.mă- ta.šak.kor- ko.nam/

نمی دونم با چه زبونی ازَتون تشکّر کنم. : 💬 🎩

/ne.mi.du.nam- bă- če- za.bu.ni- a.za.tun- ta.šak.kor- ko.nam/

I don't know how to thank you.

من که کاری نکردم. : ✏️ 💬

/man- ke- kă.ri- na.kar.dam/

It was nothing.

از هدیه ی قشنگ تان سپاسگزارم. : ✏️ 🎩

/az- had.ye.ye- ğa.šan.ge.tăn- se.păs.go.ză.ram/

از هدیه ی قشنگ تون ممنونم. : 🎩 💬

/az- had.ye.ye- ğa.šan.ge.tun- mam.nu.nam/

Thank you for the beautiful gift.

خوشحالم که پسندیده اید. : ✏️

/ǩoš.hă.lam- ke- pa.san.di.de.id/

خوشحالم که پسندیدین. : 💬

/ǩoš.hă.lam- ke- pa.san.di.dinin/

I'm glad you liked it.

نمی دانم چطور محبّتَت را جبران کنم. : ✏️

/ne.mi.dă.nam- če.tor- mo.hab.ba.tat- ră- job.răn- ko.nam/

نمی دونم چطور محبّتت رو جبران کنم. : 💬

/ne.mi.du.nam- če.tor- mo.hab.ba.tet- ră- job.răn- ko.nam/

I don't know how to return your favor.

حرفَش را هم نزن. : ✏️

/har.faš- ră- ham- na.zan/

حرفشو هم نزن. : 💬

/har.fe.šo- ham- na.zan/

Don't mention it.

✏️🗝️ : تا ابد مدیون محبّت هایتان هستم.

/tă- a.bad- mad.yu.ne- mo.hab.bat.hă.ye.tăn- has.tam/

💬🗝️ : تا ابد مدیون محبّتاتونم.

/tă- a.bad- mad.yu.ne- mo.hab.ba.ta.tu.nam/

I will be indebted to you for your kindness forever.

💬✏️ : کار خاصّی نکردم.

/kă.re- ǩăs.si- na.kar.dam/

I did nothing out of the ordinary for you.

ℹ️🗝️✏️ : چه گُل های قشنگی! خیلی ما را خجالت دادید.

/če- gol.hă.ye- ğa.šan.gi- ǩey.li- mă- ră- ǩe.jă.lat- dă.did/

ℹ️🗝️💬 : چه گُلای قشنگی! خیلی خجالت مون دادین.

/če- go.lă.ye- ğa.šan.gi- ǩey.li- ǩe.jă.la.te.mun- dă.din/

What beautiful flowers! We are so grateful.

✏️ : فقط می خواستم بدانید که به یادتان هستم.

/fa.ğat- mi.ǩăs.tam- be.dă.nid- ke- be- yă.de.tăn- has.tam/

💬 : فقط می خواستم بدونین که به یادتون هستم.

/fa.ğat- mi.ǩăs.tam- be.du.nin- ke- be- yă.de.tun- has.tam/

I just wanted you to know that I was thinking of you.

ℹ️🗝️✏️ : زحمت کشیدید، دست تان درد نکند!

/zah.mat- ke.ši.did- das.te.tăn- dard- na.ko.nad/

ℹ️🗝️💬 : زحمت کشیدین. دست تون درد نکنه!

/zah.mat- ke.ši.din- das.te.tun- dard- na.ko.ne/

You went through too much trouble. Thank you very much!

🗝️✏️ : اصلاً قابل شما را ندارد.

/as.lan- ğă.be.le- šo.mă- ră- na.dă.rad/

🗝️💬 : اصلاً قابل شما رو نداره.

/as.lan- ğă.be.le- šo.mă- ro- na.dă.re/

It is only what you deserve.

✏️ 🗣️ ⓘ : نمی خواستیم شما را به زحمت بیندازیم!

/ne.mi.kǎs.tim- šo.mǎ- rǎ- be- zah.mat- bi.yan.dǎ.zim/

💬 ✏️ 🗣️ ⓘ : نمی خواستیم شما رو به زحمت بندازیم!

/ne.mi.kǎs.tim- šo.mǎ- ro- be- zah.mat- ben.dǎ.zim/

We didn't mean to cause so much trouble for you!

✏️ 💬 : هیچ زحمتی نبود.

/hič- zah.ma.ti- na.bud/

It wasn't any trouble at all.

✏️ : چه غذای خوشمزه ای پخته ای!

/če- ǧa.zǎ.ye- kǒš.ma.ze.i- pok.te.i/

💬 : چه غذای خوشمزه ای پختی!

/če- ǧa.zǎ.ye- kǒš.ma.ze.i- pok.ti/

What delicious food you made!

✏️ ⓘ : نوش جان!

/nu.še- jǎn/

💬 ⓘ : نوش جون!

/nu.še- jun/

Enjoy!

Residence

✎ : چند وقت است اینجایید؟

/čand- vaǧt- ast- in.jă.yid/

💬 : چند وقته اینجایین؟

/čand- vaǧ.te- in.jă.yin/

How long have you been here?

✎ : سه سالی می شود که اینجا هستم.

/se- să.li- mi.ša.vad- ke- in.jă- has.tam/

💬 : سه سالی می شه که اینجام.

/se- să.li- mi.še- ke- in.jăm/

I have been here for almost three years.

✎ : خیلی وقت است آمده اید؟

/ǩey.li- vaǧt- ast- ă.ma.de.id/

💬 : خیلی وقته اومدین؟

/ǩey.li- vaǧ.te- u.ma.din/

Has it been long since you came?

✎ : نه. دو ماه بیشتر نیست.

/na- do- măh- biš.tar- nist/

💬 : نه. دو ماه بیشتر نیس.

/na- do- măh- biš.tar- nis/

No. It's only two months.

✏️ : زیاد می مانید؟

/zi.yăd- mi.mă.nid/

💬 : زیاد می مونین؟

/zi.yăd- mi.mu.nin/

Are you staying long?

✏️ : نه. فقط دو هفته اینجا هستم.

/na- fa.ğat- do- haf.te- in.jă- has.tam/

💬 : نه. فقط دو هفته اینجام.

/na- fa.ğat- do- haf.te- in.jăm/

No. I will stay only for two weeks.

✏️ : چند سال است در این شهر زندگی می کنید؟

/čand- săl- ast- dar- in- šahr- zen.de.gi- mi.ko.nid/

💬 : چند ساله توی این شهر زندگی می کنین؟

/čand- să.le- tu.ye- in- šahr- zen.de.gi- mi.ko.nin/

For how many years have you been living in this town?

✏️ : سه سال است که در این شهر زندگی می کنم.

/se- săl- ast- ke- dar- in- šahr- zen.de.gi- mi.ko.nam/

💬 : سه ساله که توی این شهر زندگی می کنم.

/se- să.le- ke- tu.ye- in- šahr- zen.de.gi- mi.ko.nam/

I have been living in this town for three years.

✏️ : تازه اسباب کشی کرده اید؟

/tă.ze- as.băb.ke.ši- kar.de.id/

💬 : تازه اسباب کشی کردین؟

/tă.ze- as.băb.ke.ši- kar.din/

Have you moved recently?

✏️ : یک ماهی می شود.

/yek- mă.hi- mi.ša.vad/

💬 : یه ماهی می شه.

/ye- mă.hi- mi.še/

It's been about a month.

✏️ : با این منطقه آشنا هستید؟

/bǎ- in- mǎn.ta.ǧe- ǎ.še.nǎ- has.tid/

💬 : با این منطقه آشنا هستین؟

/bǎ- in- man.ta.ǧe- ǎš.nǎ- has.tin/

Are you familiar with this area?

✏️ : بله، این منطقه را خیلی خوب می شناسم.

/ba.le- in- man.ta.ǧe- rǎ- ǩey.li- ǩub- mi.še.nǎ.sam/

💬 : بله. این منطقه رو خیلی خوب می شناسم.

/ba.le- in- man.ta.ǧa.ro- ǩey.li- ǩub- miš.nǎ.sam/

Yes. I know this area very well.

✏️ : قبلاً کجا زندگی می کردید؟

/ǧab.lan- ko.jǎ- zen.de.gi- mi.kar.did/

💬 : قبلاً کجا زندگی می کردین؟

/ǧab.lan- ko.jǎ- zen.de.gi- mi.kar.did/

Where were you living before?

✏️ : من قبلاً در پاریس زندگی می کردم.

/man- ǧab.lan- dar- pǎ.ris- zen.de.gi- mi.kar.dam/

💬 : من قبلاً تو پاریس زندگی می کردم.

/man- ǧab.lan- tu- pǎ.ris- zen.de.gi- mi.kar.dam/

I used to live in Paris.

✏️ : این محلّه را دوست دارید؟

/in- ma.hal.le- rǎ- dust- dǎ.rid/

💬 : این محلّه رو دوس دارین؟

/in- ma.hal.la.ro- dus- dǎ.rin/

Do you like this neighborhood?

✏️ : خیلی. من در این محلّه به دنیا آمده ام.

/ǩey.li- man- dar- in- ma.hal.le- be- don.yǎ- ǎ.ma.de.am/

💬 : خیلی. من تو این محلّه به دنیا اومدم.

/ǩey.li- man- tu- in- ma.hal.le- be- don.yǎ- u.ma.dam/

Very much. I was born in this neighborhood.

Apologies

✏️ : واقعاً معذرت می خواهم!

/vă.ğe.ʼan- maʼ.ze.rat- mi.k̆ă.ham/

💬 : واقعاً معذرت می خوام!

/vă.ğe.ʼan- maʼ.ze.rat- mi.k̆ăm/

I am truly sorry!

✏️ : برای چه داری عذرخواهی می کنی؟

/ba.ră.ye- če- dă.ri- ʼozr.k̆ă.ɦi- mi.ko.ni/

💬 : برای چی داری عذرخواهی می کنی؟

/ba.ră.ye- či- dă.ri- ʼozr.k̆ă.ɦi- mi.ko.ni/

What are you apologizing for?

✏️ : من کتابَت را گم کرده ام، واقعاً متأسّفم.

/man- ke.tă.bat- ră- gom- kar.de.am- vă.ğe.ʼan- mo.te.ʼas.se.fam/

💬 : من کتابِتو گم کردم، واقعاً متأسّفم.

/man- ke.tă.be.to- gom- kar.dam- vă.ğe.ʼan- mo.te ̱.ʼas.se.fam/

I've lost your book; I'm truly sorry.

ⓘ ✏️ : اشکالی ندارد.

/eš.k̆ă.li- na.dă.rad/

ⓘ 💬 : اشکالی نداره.

/eš.k̆ă.li- na.dă.re/

It doesn't matter.

✎ : ببخشید که ناراحت تان کردم.

/be.baǩ.šid- ke- nǎ.rǎ.ha.te.tǎn- kar.dam/

💬 : ببخشید که ناراحت تون کردم.

/be.baǩ.šid- ke- nǎ.rǎ.ha.te.tun- kar.dam/

I'm sorry that I made you upset.

🔨 ✎ : احتیاجی به عذرخواهی نیست.

/eh.ti.yǎ.ji- be- 'ozr.ǩǎ.hi- nist/

🔨 💬 : احتیاجی به عذرخواهی نیس.

/eh.ti.yǎ.ji- be- 'ozr.ǩǎ.hi- nis/

You don't need to apologize.

✎ : خواهش می کنم من را ببخشید.

/ǩǎ.heš- mi.ko.nam- man- rǎ- be.baǩ.šid/

💬 : خواهش می کنم مَنو ببخشین.

/ǩǎ.heš- mi.ko.nam- ma.no- be.baǩ.šin/

Please forgive me!

✎ : خیلی وقت است که بخشیده ام.

/ǩey.li- vaǧt- ast- ke- baǩ.ši.de.am/

💬 : خیلی وقته که بخشیدم.

/ǩey.li- vaǧ.te- ke- baǩ.ši.dam/

I forgave you a long time ago.

✎ 💬 : منظورِ بدی نداشتم.

/man.zu.re- ba.di- na.dǎš.tam/

My intentions were not bad.

✎ : می دانم.

/mi.dǎ.nam/

💬 : می دونم.

/mi.du.nam/

I know.

قصدم اهانت به شما نبود. : ✒ 🎩 💬

/ğas.dam- e.hă.nat- be- šo.mă- na.bud/

I did not mean to offend you.

امّا لحنِ تان بد بود! : ✒

/am.mă- lah.ne.tăn- bad- bud/

امّا لحنِ تون بد بود! : 💬

/am.mă- lah.ne.tun- bad- bud/

But your tone was harsh!

واقعاً از حرفی که زدم پشیمانم. : ✒

/vă.ğe.'an- az- har.fi- ke- za.dam- pa.ši.mă.nam/

واقعاً از حرفی که زدم پشیمونم. : 💬

/vă.ğe.'an- az- har.fi- ke- za.dam- pa.ši.mu.nam/

I truly regret what I said.

پشیمانی کافی نیست! : ✒

/pa.ši.mă.ni- kă.fi- nist/

پشیمونی کافی نیس! : 💬

/pa.ši.mu.ni- kă.fi- nis/

Regret is not enough!

همه اش سوء تفاهم است. : ✒

/ha.me.aš- su.'e.ta.fă.hom- ast/

همَش سوءِ تفاهمه. : 💬

/ha.maš- su.'e.ta.fă.ho.me/

This is all a misunderstanding.

امیدوارم واقعاً همینطور باشد! : ✒

/o.mid.vă.ram- vă.ğe.'an- ha.min.tor- bă.šad/

امیدوارم واقعاً همینطور باشه! : 💬

/o.mid.vă.ram- vă.ğe.'an- ha.min.tor- bă.še/

I hope you are right!

🖉 💬 : من اشتباه کردم.

/man- eš.te.bǎh- kar.dam/

I made a mistake.

💬 : نه. تو هیچ اشتباهی نکردی.

/na- to- hič- eš.te.bǎ.hi- na.kar.di/

No. You didn't make any mistake.

🖉 : نمی دانستم اینطوری می شود.

/ne.mi.dǎ.nes.tam- in.to.ri- mi.ša.vad/

💬 : نمی دونستم اینطوری می شه.

/ne.mi.du.nes.tam- in.to.ri- mi.še/

I didn't know this would happen!

🖉 : مهم نیست. خودَت را اذیت نکن.

/mo.hem- nist- ǩo.dat- rǎ- azi.yat- na.kon/

💬 : مهم نیس. خودِتو اذیت نکن.

/mo.hem- nis- ǩo.de.to- azi.yat- na.kon/

It's not a big deal. Don't beat up on yourself.

🖉 💬 : خطا از من بود.

/ǩa.tǎ- az- man- bud/

It was my mistake.

🖉 : مسأله ای نیست.

/mas.'a.le.i- nist/

💬 : مسأله ای نیس.

/mas.'a.le.i- nis/

It's not a big deal.

✏️ 💬 : تقصیر از من بود.

/tağ.sir- az- man- bud/

It was my fault.

✏️ 💬 : تقصیر از هر دوی ما بود.

/tağ.sir- az- har- do.ye- mă- bud/

We both are at fault.

✏️ : چطور می توانم جبران کنم؟

/če.tor- mi.ta.vă.nam- job.răn- ko.nam/

💬 : چطور می توونم جبران کنم؟

/če.tor- mi.tu.nam- job.răn- ko.nam/

How can I make up for it?

✏️ : عذرخواهی تان کافی بود.

/'ozr.ḱă.hi.tăn- kă.fi- bud/

💬 : عذرخواهی تون کافی بود.

/'ozr.ḱă.hi.tun- kă.fi- bud/

Your apology was enough.

ⓘ ✏️ : چطور می توانم از دلَت در بیاورم؟

/če.tor- mi.ta.vă.nam- az- de.lat- dar- bi.yă.va.ram/

ⓘ 💬 : چطور می توونم از دلت در بیارم؟

/če.tor- mi.tu.nam- az- de.let- dar- bi.yă.ram/

How can I make it up to you?

✏️ : من از تو دلخور نیستم.

/man- az-to- del.ḱor- nis.tam/

💬 : من ازَت دلخور نیستم.

/man- a.zat- del.ḱor- nis.tam/

I am not upset with you.

✏️ ⛏️ : ما را به بزرگواری خودتان ببخشید.

/mă- ră- be- bo.zorg̱.vă.ri.ye- ḱo.de.tăn- be.baḱ.šid/

💬 ⛏️ : ما رو به بزرگواری خودتون ببخشین.

/mă- ro- be- bo.zorg̱.vă.ri.ye- ḱo.de.tun- be.baḱ.šin/

Please forgive us out of the goodness of your heart.

✏️ : نمی توانم ببخشم.

/ne.mi.ta.vă.nam- be.baḱ.šam/

💬 : نمی توونم ببخشم.

/ne.mi.tu.nam- be.baḱ.šam/

I can't forgive you.

✏️ : مطمئن باشید دیگر تکرار نخواهد شد.

/mot.ma.'en- bă.šid- di.gar- tek.răr- na.ḱă.had- šod/

💬 : مطمئن باشین دیگه تکرار نمی شه.

/mot.ma.'en- bă.šin- di.ge- tek.răr- ne.mi.še/

I assure you this won't happen again.

✏️ : واقعاً امیدوارم همینطور باشد که می گویید.

/vă.ğe.'an- o.mid.vă.ram- ha.min.tor- bă.šad- ke- mi.gu.yid/

💬 : واقعاً امیدوارم همینطور باشه که می گین.

/vă.ğe.'an- o.mid.vă.ram- ha.min.tor- bă.še- ke- mi.gin/

I truly hope it's as you say.

✏️ : نمی خواستم به تو توهین کنم.

/ne.mi.ḱăs.tam- be- to- to.hin- ko.nam/

💬 : نمی خواستم بهت توهین کنم.

/ne.mi.ḱăs.tam- be.het- to.hin- ko.nam/

I didn't want to insult you.

💬 ✏️ : امّا کردی!

/am.mă- kar.di/

But you did!

112

من از طرف برادرم از شما معذرت می خواهم. : 🖉

/man- az- ta.ra.fe- ba.rǎ.da.ram- az- šo.mǎ- maʿ.ze.rat- mi.kǎ.ham/

من از طرف برادرم اَزَتون معذرت می خوام. : 💬

/man- az- ta.ra.fe- ba.rǎ.da.ram- a.za.tun- maʿ.ze.rat- mi.kǎm/

I apologize on behalf of my brother.

مسأله ای نیست. : 🖉

/mas.ʿa.le.i- nist/

مسأله ای نیس. : 💬

/mas.ʿa.le.i- nis/

It's not a big deal.

Traveling

✐ : دفعه ی اوّل است که به آمریکا می آیید؟

/daf.'e.ye- av.val- ast- ke- be- ăm.ri.kă- mi.ă.yid/

💬 : دفعه ی اوّله که میاین آمریکا؟

/daf.'e.ye- av.va.le- ke- mi.yăyn- ăm.ri.kă/

Is this your first trip to the U.S.?

✐ : بله. دفعه ی اوّل است.

/ba.le- daf.'e.ye- av.val- ast/

💬 : بله. دفعه ی اوّله.

/ba.le- daf.'e.ye- av.va.le/

Yes. It's my first time.

✐ : مسافرتِ تان تفریحی است یا تجاری؟

/mo.să.fe.ra.te.tăn- taf.ri.hist- yă- te.jă.ri/

💬 : مسافرتِ تون تفریحیه یا تجاری؟

/mo.să.fe.ra.te.tun- taf.ri.hi.ye- yă- te.jă.ri/

Are you traveling for business or pleasure?

✐ : مسافرتم فقط برایِ تفریح است.

/mo.să.fe.ra.tam- fa.ğat- ba.ră.ye- taf.rih- ast/

💬 : مسافرتم فقط برایِ تفریحه.

/mo.să.fe.ra.tam- fa.ğat- ba.ră.ye- taf.ri.he/

I am traveling only for pleasure.

✏️ : خیال دارید چقدر بمانید؟

/ǩi.yǎl- dǎ.rid- če.ğadr- be.mǎ.nid/

💬 : خیال دارین چقدر بمونین؟

/ǩi.yǎl- dǎ.rin- če.ğadr- be.mu.nin/

How long are you planning to stay?

✏️ : خیال دارم حداقل دو ماه اینجا بمانم.

/ǩi.yǎl- dǎ.ram- had.de.a.ğal- do- mǎh- in.jǎ- be.mǎ.nam/

💬 : خیال دارم دست کم دو ماهی اینجا بمونم.

/ǩi.yǎl- dǎ.ram- das.te- kam- do- mǎ.hi- in.jǎ- be.mu.nam/

I'm planning to stay for at least two months.

✏️ : چه مدّت می مانید؟

/če- mod.dat- mi.mǎ.nid/

💬 : چه مدّت می مونین؟

/če- mod.dat- mi.mu.nin/

How long are you going to stay?

✏️ : یک هفته می مانم.

/yek- haf.te- mi.mǎ.nam/

💬 : یه هفته می مونم.

/ye- haf.te- mi.mu.nam/

I'll stay for a week.

✏️ : کجاها را دیده اید؟

/ko.jǎ.hǎ- rǎ- di.de.id/

💬 : کجاها رو دیدین؟

/ko.jǎ.hǎ- ro- di.din/

Which places have you seen so far?

4/9/22
Saeed

✏️ : مجسّمه ی آزادی را دیده ام.

/mo.jas.sa.me.ye- ǎ.zǎ.di- rǎ- di.de.am/

💬 : مجسّمه ی آزادی رو دیدم.

/mo.jas.sa.me.ye- ǎ.zǎ.di- ro- di.dam/

I've seen the Statue of Liberty.

✏️ توی هتل هستید؟

/tu.ye- ho.tel- has.tid/

💬 توی هتل هستین؟

/tu.ye- ho.tel- has.tin/

Are you staying in a hotel?

✏️ نه. خانه ی دوستم هستم.

/na- ǩǎ.ne.ye- dus.tam- has.tam/

💬 نه. خونه ی دوستم هستم.

/na- ǩu.ne.ye- dus.tam- has.tam/

No. I'm staying with a friend.

✏️ با ترن آمدید یا با هواپیما؟

/bǎ- te.ran- ǎ.ma.did- yǎ- bǎ- ha.vǎ.pey.mǎ/

💬 با ترن اومدین یا با هواپیما؟

/bǎ- te.ran- u.ma.din- yǎ- bǎ- ha.vǎ.pey.mǎ/

Did you come on a train or a plane?

💬 ✏️ با هواپیما.

/bǎ- ha.vǎ.pey.mǎ/

On a plane.

✏️ پروازتان چطور بود؟

/par.vǎ.ze.tǎn- če.tor- bud/

💬 پروازتون چطور بود؟

/par.vǎ.ze.tun- če.tor- bud/

How was your flight?

💬 ✏️ خیلی خوب و راحت بود.

/ǩey.li- ǩu.bo- rǎ.hat- bud/

It was very pleasant.

پرواز‌تان چند ساعت بود؟ : ✏️

/par.vă.ze.tăn- čand- să.'at- bud/

پرواز‌تون چند ساعت بود؟ : 💬

/par.vă.ze.tun- čand- să.'at- bud/

How long was your flight?

هفت ساعت و نیم. : 💬

/haft- să.'a.to- nim/

It was seven and a half hours.

پرواز‌تان مستقیم بود؟ : ✏️

/par.vă.ze.tăn- mos.ta.ğim- bud/

پرواز‌تون مستقیم بود؟ : 💬

/par.vă.ze.tun- mos.ta.ğim- bud/

Was your flight direct?

نه. پروازم یک توقّف داشت. : ✏️

/na- par.vă.zam- yek- ta.vağ.ğof- dăšt /

نه. پروازم یه توقّف داشت. : 💬

/na- par.vă.zam- ye- ta.vağ.ğof- dăšt /

No. My flight had one stop.

پرواز‌تان تأخیر هم داشت؟ : ✏️

/par.vă.ze.tăn- ta.'ḱir- ham- dăšt/

پرواز‌تون تأخیرم داشت؟ : 💬

/par.vă.ze.tun- ta.'ḱir- ham- dăšt/

Was your flight delayed?

بله. پروازم یک ساعت تأخیر داشت. : ✏️

/ba.le- par.vă.zam- yek- să.'at- ta.'ḱir- dăšt/

بله. پروازم یه ساعت تأخیر داشت. : 💬

/ba.le- par.vă.zam- ye- să.'at- ta.'ḱir- dăšt/

Yes. My flight was delayed for one hour.

✏ : توی گمرک خیلی مُعَطّل شدید؟

/tu.ye- gom.rok- ǩey.li- mo.ʼat.tal- šo.did/

💬 : توی گمرک خیلی مَعطَل شدین؟

/tu.ye- gom.rok- ǩey.li- maʼ.tal- šo.din/

Did it take long to pass through Customs?

✏ : نه. به نسبت زود از گمرک بیرون آمدم.

/na- be- nes.bat- zud- az- gom.rok- bi.run- ǎ.ma.dam/

💬 : نه. به نسبت زود از گمرگ در اومدم.

/na- be- nes.bat- zud- az- gom.rok- dar- u.ma.dam/

No. I passed through Customs relatively quickly.

✏ : از فرودگاه تا اینجا چند ساعت راه است؟

/az- fo.rud.gǎh- ta- in.jǎ- čand- sǎ.ʼat- rǎh- ast/

💬 : از فرودگاه تا اینجا چند ساعت راهه؟

/az- fo.rud.gǎh- ta- in.jǎ- čand- sǎ.ʼat- rǎ.he/

How long does it take to get here from the airport?

💬 ✏ : سه ساعت و بیست دقیقه.

/se- sǎ.ʼa.to- bist- da.ǧi.ǧe/

Three hours and twenty minutes.

✏ : ماشین هم کرایه کردید؟

/mǎ.šin- ham- ke.rǎ.ye- kar.did/

💬 : ماشینَم کرایه کردین؟

/mǎ.ši.nam- ke.rǎ.ye- kar.din/

Did you rent a car too?

💬 ✏ : نه، اتوبوس سوار شدیم.

/na- o.to.bus- sa.vǎr- šo.dim/

No, we took the bus.

✏ : هتل را از قبل رزرو کردید؟

/ho.tel- ră- az- ğabl- re.zerv- kar.did/

💬 : هتلو از قبل رزرو کردین؟

/ho.te.lo- az- ğabl- re.zerv- kar.din/

Did you make a reservation for the hotel in advance?

✏ : بله. هتل را حتماً باید از دو ماه قبل رزرو کرد.

/ba.le- ho.tel- ră- hat.man- bă.yad- az- do- mă.he- ğabl- re.zerv- kard/

💬 : بله. هتلو حتماً باید از دو ماه قبل رزرو کرد.

/ba.le- ho.te.lo- hat.man- bă.yad- az- do- măh- ğabl- re.zerv- kard/

Yes. You certainly need to reserve the hotel at least two months in advance.

✏ : تعطیلات عید کجا رفتید؟

/ta'.ti.lă.te- 'eyd- ko.jă- raf.tid/

💬 : تعطیلات عید کجا رفتین؟

/ta'.ti.lă.te- 'eyd- ko.jă- raf.tin/

Where did you go for Norooz Holidays?

✏ : هیچ کجا. بلیت گیر نیاوَردیم.

/hič- ko.jă- be.lit- gir- na.yă.var.dim/

💬 : هیچ جا. بلیت گیر نیاوُردیم.

/hič- jă- be.lit- gir- na.yă.vor.dim/

Nowhere. We couldn't get tickets.

Invitations

✏️ : می خواستم شما را برای تولّدم دعوت کنم.

/mi.kǎs.tam- šo.mǎ- rǎ- ba.rǎ.ye- ta.val.lo.dam- daʻ.vat- ko.nam/

💬 : می خواستم شما رو برای تولّدم دعوت کنم.

/mi.kǎs.tam- šo.mǎ- ro- ba.rǎ.ye- ta.val.lo.dam- daʻ.vat- ko.nam/

I would like to invite you to my birthday party.

✏️ : از دعوت تان ممنونم. تولّدِتان کِی است؟

/az- daʻ.va.te.tǎn- mam.nu.nam- ta.val.lo.de.tǎn- key- ast/

💬 : از دعوت تون ممنونم. تولّدِتون کِیه؟

/az- daʻ.va.te.tun- mam.nu.nam- ta.val.lo.de.tun- ke.ye/

Thank you for the invitation. When is your birthday?

✏️ : سه شنبه ی دیگر. لطفاً دوستِ تان را هم از طرفِ من دعوت کنید.

/se.šan.be.ye- di.gar- lot.fan- dus.te.tǎn- rǎ- ham- az- ta.ra.fe- man- daʻ.vat- ko.nid/

💬 : سه شنبه ی دیگه. لطفاً دوستِ تونَم از طرفِ من دعوت کنین.

/se.šan.be.ye- di.ge- lot.fan- dus.te.tu.nam- az- ta.ra.fe- man- daʻ.vat- ko.nin/

Next Tuesday. Please invite your friend as well on my behalf.

💬 ✏️ : حتماً. خیلی ممنون.

/hat.man- ǩey.li- mam.nun/

Sure. Thank you so much.

✏️ : ما فردا می خواهیم برویم کنار آب. اگر تو هم بیایی، خوشحال می شویم.

/mă- far.dă- mi.ǩă.him- be.ra.vim- ke.nă.re- ăb- a.gar-to- ham- bi.yǎ.yi- ǩoš.hǎl- mi.ša.vim/

💬 : ما فردا می خوایم بریم کنار آب. اگه تو هم بیای خوشحال می شیم.

/mă- far.dă- mi.ǩăym- be.rim- ke.nă.re- ăb- a.ge- to- ham- bi.yǎy- ǩoš.hǎl- mi.šim/

We want to go to the beach tomorrow. We would be happy if you would join us.

💬 ✏️ : متأسّفانه من فردا کار می کنم.

/mo.te.'as.se.fǎ.ne- man- far.dă- kǎr- mi.ko.nam/

Unfortunately, I have to work tomorrow.

✏️👔 : هفته ی دیگر تولّد من است. شما هم تشریف بیاورید.

/haf.te.ye- di.gar- ta.val.lo.de- man- ast- šo.mǎ- ham- taš.rif- bi.yǎ.va.rid/

💬👔 : هفته ی دیگه تولّدَمه. شما هم تشریف بیارین.

/haf.te.ye- di.ge- ta.val.lo.de- ma.ne- šo.mǎ- ham- taš.rif- bi.yǎ.rin/

Next week is my birthday party. Please join us.

✏️👔ⓘ : حتماً مزاحمِ تان می شویم.

/hat.man- mo.zǎ.he.me.tǎn- mi.ša.vim/

💬👔ⓘ : حتماً مزاحمِ تون می شیم.

/hat.man- mo.zǎ.he.me.tun- mi.šim/

We definitely will.

✏️ : شب سال نو، همگی خانه ی ما دعوت دارید. جای دیگر قول ندهید.

/ša.be- sǎ.le- no- ha.me.gi- ǩă.ne.ye- mǎ- da'.vat- dǎ.rid- jǎ.ye- di.gar- ǧol- na.da.hid/

💬 : شب سال نو، همگی خونه ی ما دعوت دارین. جای دیگه قول ندین.

/ša.be- sǎ.le- no- ha.me.gi- ǩu.ne.ye- mǎ- da'.vat- dǎ.rin- jǎ.ye- di.ge- ǧol- na.din/

All of you are invited to our place for New Year's Eve. Don't make other plans.

✏️ : باشد.

/bǎ.šad/

💬 : باشه.

/bǎ.še/

O.k.

فردا با هم برویم بیرون. : ✎

/far.dă- bă- ham- be.ra.vim- bi.run/

فردا با هم بریم بیرون. : 💬

/far.dă- bă- ham- be.rim- bi.run/

Let's go out tomorrow.

فردا گرفتارم. یکشنبه ها برایَم بهترست. : ✎

/far.dă- ge.ref.tă.ram- yek.šan.be.hă- ba.ră.yam- beh.ta.rast/

فردا گرفتارم. یکشنبه ها برام بهتره. : 💬

/far.dă- ge.ref.tă.ram- yek.šan.be.hă- ba.răm- beh.ta.re/

I am busy tomorrow. Sundays work better for me.

ناهار می مانی؟ : ✎

/nă.hăr- mi.mă.ni/

ناهار می مونی؟ : 💬

/nă.hăr- mi.mu.ni/

Will you stay for lunch?

نه نمی توانم بمانم. انشاء الله یک وقت دیگر. : ✎

/na- ne.mi.ta.vă.nam- be.mă.nam- en.šă.al.lăh- yek- vağ.te- di.gar/

نه نمی توونم بمونم. ایشالاّ یه وقت دیگه. : 💬

/na- ne.mi.tu.nam- be.mu.nam- i.šăl.lă- ye- vağ.te- di.ge/

No, I can't. Hopefully (God willing) another time.

وقت داری با هم قهوه بخوریم؟ : ✎ 💬

/vağt- dă.ri- bă- ham- ğah.ve- be.ǩo.rim/

Do you have time to have coffee with me?

آره. نیم ساعتی وقت دارم. : ✎ 💬

/ă.re- nim- să.ʿa.ti- vağt- dă.ram/

Yes. I have half an hour to spare.

✎ : دوشنبه مراسمِ فارغ التحصیلیِ من است. می آیی؟

/do.šan.be- ma.rǎ.se.me- fǎ.reǧ.ǧo.tah.si.li.ye- man- ast- mi.ǎ.yi/

💬 : دوشنبه مراسمِ فارغ التحصیلیِ منه. میای؟

/do.šan.be- ma.rǎ.se.me- fǎ.reǧ.ǧo.tah.si.li.ye- ma.ne- mi.yǎy/

Monday is my graduation ceremony. Will you come?

✎ : معلوم است که می آیم.

/ma'.lum- ast- ke- mi.ǎ.yam/

💬 : معلومه که میام.

/ma'.lu.me- ke- mi.yǎm/

Of course I will.

✎ : هر وقت به شهر آمدی، به دیدن من بیا.

/har- vaǧt- be- šahr- ǎ.ma.di- be- di.da.ne- man- bi.yǎ/

💬 : هروقت اومدی شهر، بیا دیدنِ من.

/har- vaǧt- u.ma.di- šahr- bi.yǎ- di.da.ne- man/

Whenever you are in town, pay me a visit.

✎ 💬 : حتماً.

/hat.man/

Sure thing.

Memories

✏️ : یادَت هست ده سال پیش این آپارتمانِ ها چقدر ارزان بودند؟

/yǎ.dat- hast- dah- sǎ.le- piš- in- ǎ.pǎr.te.mǎn.hǎ- če.ğadr- ar.zǎn- bu.dand/

💬 : یادته ده سال پیش این آپارتمانا چقدر ارزون بودن؟

/yǎ.de.te- dah- sǎ.le- piš- in- ǎ.pǎr.te.mǎ.nǎ- če.ğadr- ar.zun- bu.dan/

Do you remember how inexpensive these apartments were ten years ago?

✏️ : آره. خوب یادم است.

/ǎ.re- ǩub- yǎ.dam- ast/

💬 : آره. خوب یادمه.

/ǎ.re- ǩub- yǎ.da.me/

Yes. I remember it perfectly.

✏️ : پارسال مهمانیِ سام چقدر به ما خوش گذشت!

/pǎr.sǎl- meh.mǎ.ni.ye- sǎm- če.ğadr- be- mǎ- ǩoš- go.zašt/

💬 : پارسال مهمونیِ سام چقدر به ما خوش گذشت!

/pǎr.sǎl- meh.mu.ni.ye- sǎm- če.ğadr- be- mǎ- ǩoš- go.zašt/

What a wonderful time we had last year at Sam's party!

✏️💬 : به ما هم همینطور.

/be- mǎ- ham- ha.min.tor/

We had a good time too.

Memories

چه روزگارِ خوبی بود! : 🖉 💬

/če- ru.ze.gă.re- ǩu.bi- bud/

Those were the good old days!

کاشکی آن روزها دوباره برمی گشتند! : 🖉

/kăš.ki- ăn- ruz.hă- do.bă.re- bar.mi.gaš.tand/

کاشکی اون روزا دوباره برمی گشتن! : 💬

/kăš.ki- un- ru.ză- do.bă.re- bar.mi.gaš.tan/

I wish those days could have lasted forever!

یادَش بخیر! آنوقت ها چقدر انرژی داشتیم! : 🖉

/yă.daš- be.ǩeyr- ăn.vağt.hă- če.ğadr- e.ner.ži- dăš.tim/

یادش بخیر! اونوقتا چقدر انرژی داشتیم! : 💬

/yă.deš- be.ǩeyr- un.vağ.tă- če.ğadr- e.ner.ži- dăš.tim/

We used to have so much energy! Good old times!

خُب، خیلی جوان تر بودیم. : 🖉

/ǩob- ǩey.li- ja.văn.tar- bu.dim/

خُب، خیلی جوون تر بودیم. : 💬

/ǩob- ǩey.li- ja.vun.tar- bu.dim/

Well, we were much younger!

باورَت می شود که بیست سال از دوران دانشکده گذشته است؟ : 🖉

/bă.va.rat- mi.šă.vad- ǩe- bist- săl- az- do.ră.ne- dă.neš.ka.de- go.zaš.te- ast/

باورت می شه که بیست سال از دوران دانشکده گذشته؟ : 💬

/bă.va.ret- mi.šě- ke- bist- săl- az- do.ră.ne- dă.neš.ka.de- go.zaš.te/

Can you believe it's been twenty years since college?

چقدر زمان زود می گُذرد. : 🖉

/če.ğadr- za.măn- zud- mi.go.za.rad/

چقدر زمان زود می گذره. : 💬

/če.ğadr- za.măn- zud- mig.za.re/

Time flies!

✏ : هیچوقت یادم نمی رود چقدر سام در آن سفر به ما محبّت کرد!

/hič.vaĝt- yă.dam- ne.mi.ra.vad- če.ĝadr- săm- dar- ăn- sa.far- be- mă- mo.hab.bat- kard/

💬 : هیچوقت یادم نمی ره چقدر سام توی اون سفر به ما محبّت کرد!

/hič.vaĝt- yă.dam- ne.mi.re- če.ĝadr- săm- tu.ye- un- sa.far- be- mă- mo.hab.bat- kard/

I will never forget how kind Sam was to us during that trip!

💬 ✏ : آره، خیلی خوش گذشت!

/ă.re- ķey.li- ķoš- go.zašt/

Yes. We had a really good time!

Suggestions & Advice

✏️ : فکر می کنی من باید راجع به این مسأله چه کار کنم؟

/fekr- mi.ko.ni- man- bǎ.yad- rǎ.je'- be- in- mas.'a.le- če- kǎr- ko.nam/

💬 : فکر می کنی من باید راجبِ این مسأله چه کار کنم؟

/fekr- mi.ko.ni- man- bǎ.yad- rǎ.je.be- in- mas.'a.le- če- kǎr- ko.nam/

What do you think I should do about this issue?

💬 ✏️ : با عجله تصمیم نگیر.

/bǎ- 'a.ja.le- tas.mim- na.gir/

Don't make a rushed decision.

✏️ : نظرِ تو چیست؟

/na.za.re- to- čist/

💬 : نظرِ تو چیه؟

/na.za.re- to- či.ye/

What do you think?

✏️ : به نظرِ من بهترست یک امتحانی بکنی.

/be- na.za.re- man- beh.ta.rast- yek- em.te.hǎ.ni- be.ko.ni/

💬 : به نظرِ من بهتره یه امتحانی بکنی.

/be- na.za.re- man- beh.ta.re- ye- em.te.hǎ.ni- be.ko.ni/

I think you should give it a try.

✎ : بنظرَت چطور می آید؟
/be.na.za.rat- če.tor- mi.ă.yad/

💬 : بنظرت چطور میاد؟
/be.na.za.ret- če.tor- mi.yăd/

How does it seem to you?

✎ : بنظر من جالب است.
/be.na.za.re- man- jă.leb- ast/

💬 : بنظر من جالبه.
/be.na.za.re- man- jă.le.be/

It seems interesting to me.

✎ : بنظرَت منطقی است؟
/be.ne.na.za.rat- man.te.ği- ast/

💬 : بنظرت منطقیه؟
/be.ne.na.za.ret- man.te.ği.ye/

Does it sound rational to you?

✎ : نه. اصلاً منطقی نیست.
/na- as.lan- man.te.ği- nist/

💬 : نه. اصلاً منطقی نیس.
/na- as.lan- man.te.ği- nis/

No. This is not rational at all.

✎ : اگر تو جای من بودی چه کار می کردی؟
/a.gar- to- jă.ye- man- bu.di- če- kăr- mi.kar.di/

💬 : اگه تو جای من بودی چی کار می کردی؟
/a.ge- to- jă.ye- man- bu.di- či- kăr- mi.kar.di/

What would you do if you were in my situation?

✎ : من اگر جای تو بودم، حتماً از آنها شکایت می کردم.
/man- a.gar- jă.ye- to- bu.dam- hat.man- az- ăn.hă- še.kă.yat- mi.kar.dam/

💬 : من اگه جای تو بودم، حتماً ازشون شکایت می کردم.
/man- a.ge- jă.ye- to- bu.dam- hat.man- a.za.šun- še.kă.yat- mi.kar.dam/

If I were you, I would file a complaint.

128

✏️ : پیشنهادِ تو چیست؟

/piš.na.hǎ.de- to- čist/

💬 : پیشنهادِ تو چیه؟

/piš.na.hǎ.de- to- či.ye/

What is your suggestion?

💬 ✏️ : من پیشنهادی ندارم.

/man- piš.na.hǎ.di- na.dǎ.ram/

I have no suggestions.

✏️ : می خواستم با تو راجع به مسأله ای مشورت کنم.

/mi.kǎs.tam- bǎ- to- rǎ.je'- be- mas.'a.le.i- maš.ve.rat- ko.nam/

💬 : می خواستم باهات راجبِ مسأله ای مشورت کنم.

/mi.kǎs.tam- bǎ.hǎt- rǎ.je.be- mas.'a.le.i- maš.ve.rat- ko.nam/

I want to seek your advice about an issue.

✏️ : باشد. موضوع چیست؟

/bǎ.šad- mo.zu'- čist/

💬 : باشه. موضوع چیه؟

/bǎ.še- mo.zu'- či.ye/

O.k. What is the matter?

💬 ✏️ : احتیاج به کمکِ فکریِ تو دارم.

/eh.ti.yǎj- be- ko.ma.ke- fek.ri.ye- to- dǎ.ram/

I need to pick your brain.

✏️ : بگو، گوش می دهم.

/be.gu- guš- mi.da.ham/

💬 : بگو، گوش می دَم.

/be.gu- guš- mi.dam/

Tell me, I'm listening.

باید با یک نفر حرف بزنم! : ✐

/bă.yad- bă- yek- na.far- harf- be.za.nam/

باید با یه نفر حرف بزنم! : 💬

/bă.yad- bă- ye- na.far- harf- be.za.nam/

I need to talk to someone!

با من می توانی حرف بزنی. : ✐

/bă- man- mi.ta.vă.ni- harf- be.za.ni/

با من می توونی حرف بزنی. : 💬

/bă- man- mi.tu.ni- harf- be.za.ni/

You can talk to me!

به من کمک می کنی تصمیمَم را بگیرم؟ : ✐

/be- man- ko.mak- mi.ko.ni- tas.mi.mam- ră- be.gi.ram/

به من کمک می کنی تصمیمَمو بگیرم؟ : 💬

/be- man- ko.mak- mi.ko.ni- tas.mi.ma.mo- be.gi.ram/

Would you help me make up my mind?

نه، خودَت باید تصمیم بگیری. : ✐

/na- ǩo.dat- bă.yad- tas.mim- be.gi.ri/

نه، خودت باید تصمیم بگیری. : 💬

/na- ǩo.det- bă.yad- tas.mim- be.gi.ri/

No. You have to make this decision on your own.

تو می گویی چه کار کنم؟ : ✐

/to- mi.gu.yi- če- kăr- ko.nam/

تو می گی چی کار کنم؟ : 💬

/to- mi.gi- či- kăr- ko.nam/

What do you suggest I do?

من می گویم حقیقت را به او بگو. : ✐

/man- mi.gu.yam- ha.ǧi.ǧat- ră- be- u- be.gu/

من می گم حقیقَتو بِهش بگو. : 💬

/man- mi.gam- ha.ǧi.ǧa.to- be.heš- be.gu/

I suggest that you tell him/her the truth.

بین خودمان باشد، اصلاً نمی دانم چه کار کنم. : 🖉

/bey.ne- ǩo.de.mǎn- bǎ.šad- as.lan- ne.mi.dǎ.nam- če- kǎr- ko.nam/

بین خودمون باشه، اصلاً نمی دونم چی کار کنم. : 💬

/bey.ne- ǩo.de.mun- bǎ.še- as.lan- ne.mi.du.nam- či- kǎr- ko.nam/

Between you and me, I have no idea what to do.

سخت نگیر. حل خواهد شد. 🖉

/saǩt- na.gir- hal- ǩǎ.had- šod/

سخت نگیر. حل می شه. 💬

/saǩt- na.gir- hal- mi.še/

Take it easy. It will be o.k.

یک راه حلّی جلوی پای من بگُذار! : ①🖉

/yek- rǎ.he- hal.li- je.lo.ye- pǎ.ye- man- be.go.zǎr/

یه راه حلّی جلوی پای من بذار! : ①💬

/ye- rǎ.he- hal.li- je.lo.ye- pǎ.ye- man- be.zǎr/

Show me the way!

هیچ راه حلّی به ذهنم نمی رسد. : ①🖉

/hič- rǎ.he- hal.li- be- zeh.nam- ne.mi.re.sad/

هیچ راه حلّی به ذهنم نمی رسه. : ①💬

/hič- rǎ.he- hal.li- be- zeh.nam- ne.mi.re.se/

I can't think of a single solution.

خودم به تنهایی از پسَش برنمی آیم. : 🖉

/ǩo.dam- be- tan.hǎ.yi- az- pa.saš- bar.ne.mi.ǎ.yam/

خودم تنهایی از پسش برنمیام. : 💬

/ǩo.dam- tan.hǎ.yi- az- pa.seš- bar.ne.mi.yǎm/

I can't handle it all by myself.

چرا، برمی آیی. : 🖉

/če.rǎ- bar.mi.ǎ.yi/

چرا، برمیای. : 💬

/če.rǎ- bar.mi.yǎy/

Of course you can.

Consolations

✏ : خیلی پشیمانم.

/ǩey.li- pa.ši.mǎ.nam/

💬 : خیلی پشیمونم.

/ǩey.li- pa.ši.mu.nam/

I regret it very much.

✏ : خودَت را ناراحت نکن.

/ǩo.dat- rǎ- nǎ.rǎ.hat- na.kon/

💬 : خودتِو ناراحت نکن.

/ǩo.de.to- nǎ.rǎ.hat- na.kon/

Don't feel bad about it.

✏💬 : همه چیز خراب شد!

/ha.me- čiz- ǩa.rǎb- šod/

Everything is ruined!

✏ : همه چیز درست می شود، من به تو قول می دهم.

/ha.me- čiz- do.rost- mi.ša.vad- man- be- to- ǧol- mi.da.ham/

💬 : همه چیز درست می شه، من بِهت قول می دم.

/ha.me- čiz- do.rost- mi.še- man- be.het- ǧol- mi.dam/

Everything is going to be alright, I promise you.

✏️ 💬 : خیلی نگرانم.

/ǩey.li- ne.ga.rǎ.nam/

I am so worried.

✏️ : جای نگرانی نیست.

/jǎ.ye- ne.ga.rǎ.ni- nist/

💬 : جای نگرانی نیس.

/jǎ.ye- ne.ga.rǎ.ni- nis/

There is nothing to be worried about.

✏️ : راستَش را بگو، تو چه فکر می کنی؟

/rǎs.taš- rǎ- be.gu- to- če- fekr- mi.ko.ni/

💬 : راستشو بگو، تو چی فکر می کنی؟

/rǎs.te.šo- be.gu- to- či- fekr- mi.ko.ni/

Tell me the truth, what do you think?

✏️ : مسأله آنقدر هم اساسی نیست.

/mas.'a.le- ǎn.ğadr- ham- a.sǎ.si- nist/

💬 : مسأله اونقدرَم اساسی نیس.

/mas.'a.le- un.ğad.ram- a.sǎ.si- nis/

It's not that big of a deal.

✏️ : این مشکل درست شدنی نیست!

/in- moš.kel- do.rost- šo.da.ni- nist/

💬 : این مشکل درست شدنی نیس!

/in- moš.kel- do.rost- šo.da.ni- nis/

This is not a problem that can be fixed!

ℹ️ ✏️ : بزرگَش نکن.

/bo.zor.gaš- na.kon/

💬 ℹ️ : بزرگِش نکن.

/bo.zor.geš- na.kon/

Don't exaggerate.

✏️ : وضع خیلی خراب است!

/vaz' - ǩey.li- ǩa.răb- ast/

💬 : وضع خیلی خرابه!

/vaz' - ǩey.li- ǩa.ră.be/

It looks pretty bad.

✏️ : اوضاع آنقدر هم که فکر می کنی بد نیست.

/o.ză' - ăn.ğadr- ham- ke- fekr- mi.ko.ni- bad- nist/

💬 : اوضاع اونقدرَم که فکر می کنی بد نیس.

/o.ză' - un.ğad.ram- ke- fekr- mi.ko.ni- bad- nis/

Things are not as bad as you think.

✏️ : حالا می گویی چه کار کنم؟

/hă.lă- mi.gu.yi- če- kăr- ko.nam/

💬 : حالا می گی چی کار کنم؟

/hă.lă- mi.gi- či- kăr- ko.nam/

What would you suggest I do now?

✏️ : خونسردی ات را حفظ کن.

/ǩun.sar.di.at- ră- hefz- kon/

💬 : خونسردیت رو حفظ کن.

/ǩun.sar.dit- ro- hefz- kon/

Keep your cool.

✏️ : دارم دیوانه می شوم!

/dă.ram- di.vă.ne- mi.ša.vam/

💬 : دارم دیوونه می شَم!

/dă.ram- di.vu.ne- mi.šam/

I'm going nuts!

✏️ : صبور باش! سختی اش گذشته است.

/sa.bur- băš- saǩ.ti.aš- go.zaš.te- ast/

💬 : صبور باش! سختیش گذشته.

/sa.bur- băš- saǩ.tiš- go.zaš.te/

Be patient, the worst is over.

✏️ 💬 : تصادف خیلی بدی بود! ماشینم داغون شد!

/ta.să.do.fe- ǩey.li- ba.di- bud- mă.ši.nam- dă.ğun- šod/

It was a very bad accident! My car is a wreck!

✏️ : می توانست خیلی بدتر از اینها بشود.

/mi.ta.vă.nest- ǩey.li- bad.tar- az- in.hă- be.ša.vad/

💬 : می توونست خیلی بدتر از اینا بشه.

/mi.tu.nest- ǩey.li- bad.tar- az- i.nă- be.še/

It could have been much worse.

✏️ : رئیسم دارد دیوانه ام می کند!

/ra.ʼi.sam- dă.rad- di.va.ne.am- mi.ko.nad/

💬 : رئیسم داره دیوونَم می کنه!

/ra.ʼi.sam- dă.re- di.vu.nam- mi.ko.ne/

My boss is driving me crazy!

✏️ 💬 : سخت نگیر.

/saǩt- na.gir/

Take it easy.

✏️ : خیلی افسرده ام.

/ǩey.li- af.sor.de.am/

💬 : خیلی افسردم.

/ǩey.li- af.sor.dam/

I'm very depressed.

ⓘ ✏️ : چه می گویی؟ دنیا که به آخر نرسیده است.

/če- mi.gu.yi- don.yă- ke- be- ă.ǩar- na.re.si.de- ast/

ⓘ 💬 : چی می گی؟ دنیا که به آخر نرسیده.

/či- mi.gi- don.yă- ke- be- ă.ǩar- na.re.si.de/

What are you talking about? It is not the end of the world.

شرکتم من را به کالیفرنیا منتقل کرده است! : ✏
/šer.ka.tam- man- rǎ- be- kǎ.li.for.ni.yǎ- mon.ta.ğel- kar.de- ast/

شرکتم مَنو به کالیفرنیا منتقل کرده! : 💬
/šer.ka.tam- ma.no- be- kǎ.li.for.ni.yǎ- mon.ta.ğel- kar.de/

My company has transferred me to California!

بد که نیست. جنبه ی مثبتَش را ببین. : ✏
/bad- ke- nist- jan.be.ye- mos.ba.taš- rǎ- be.bin/

بد که نیس. جنبه ی مثبتِشو ببین. : 💬
/bad- ke- nis- jan.be.ye- mos.ba.te.šo- be.bin/

That is not a bad thing. Look on the bright side.

دو ماه است از دوستم بی خبرم. : ✏
/do- mǎh- ast- az- dus.tam- bi.ǩa.ba.ram/

دو ماهه از دوستم بی خبرم. : 💬
/do- mǎ.he- az- dus.tam- bi.ǩa.ba.ram/

I haven't heard from my friend for two months.

به دلَت بد نیاوَر. : ✏ⓘ
/be- de.lat- bad- na.yǎ.var/

به دلت بد نیار. : 💬ⓘ
/be- de.lét- bad- na.yǎr/

Don't worry too much!

این سرماخوردگی دارد من را از پا می اندازد! : ✏ⓘ
/in- sar.mǎ.ǩor.de.gi- dǎ.rad- man- rǎ- az- pǎ- mi.an.dǎ.zad/

این سرماخوردگی داره مَنو از پا میندازه! : 💬ⓘ
/in- sar.mǎ.ǩor.de.gi- dǎ.re- ma.no- az- pǎ- min.dǎ.ze/

This cold is going to be the end of me!

فقط یک عطسه کرده ای، از کاه کوه نساز! : ✏ⓘ
/fa.ğat- yek- 'at.se- kar.de.i- az- kǎh- kuh- na.sǎz/

فقط یه عطسه کردی، از کاه کوه نساز! : 💬ⓘ
/fa.ğat- ye- 'at.se- kar.di- az- kǎh- kuh- na.sǎz/

It was just a sneeze. Don't blow it out of proportion!

رئیسم با من خیلی تند حرف زد!

/ra.ʼi.sam- bă- man- ǩey.li- tond- harf- zad/

My boss spoke harshly to me!

بهت بر نخورد! با همه اینطوری حرف می زند.

/be.het- bar.na.ǩo.rad- bă- ha.me- in.to.ri- harf- mi.za.nad/

بهت بر نخوره! با همه اینطوری حرف می زنه.

/be.het- bar.na.ǩo.re- bă- ha.me- in.to.ri- harf- mi.za.ne/

Don't get offended! He talks to everyone like that.

خیلی دلم برای خانه تنگ می شود!

/ǩey.li- de.lam- ba.ră.ye- ǩă.ne- tang- mi.ša.vad/

خیلی دلم برای خونه تنگ می شه!

/ǩey.li- de.lam- ba.ră.ye- ǩu.ne- tang- mi.še/

I miss home very much!

چاره ای نیست. باید دوری را تحمّل کنی!

/čă.re.i- nist- bă.yad- du.ri- ră- ta.ham.mol- ko.ni/

چاره ای نیس. باید دوری رو تحمّل کنی!

/čă.re.i- nis- bă.yad- du.ri-ro- ta.ham.mol- ko.ni/

You have no choice. You've got to bear the distance!

ای کاش می توانستیم خانه مان را عوض کنیم.

/ey- kăš- mi.ta.vă.nes.tim- ǩă.ne.măn- ră- ʼa.vaz- ko.nim/

ای کاش می توونستیم خونَمونو عوض کنیم.

/ey- kăš- mi.tu.nes.tim- ǩu.na.mu.no- ʼa.vaz- ko.nim/

I wish we could move to a new house.

فعلاً همین است که هست! کاریش نمی شود کرد!

/feʻ.lan- ha.min- ast- ke- hast- ǩă.riš- ne.mi.ša.vad- kard/

فعلاً همینه که هس! کاریش نمی شه کرد!

/feʻ.lan- ha.mi.ne- ke- has- ǩă.riš- ne.mi.še- kard/

It is what it is for now! We can't do anything about it!

بدجوری توی دردسر افتاده ام! : ⓘ ✎

/bad.ju.ri- tu.ye- dar.de.sar- of.tǎ.de.am/

بدجوری تو دردسر افتادم! : ⓘ 💬

/bad.ju.ri- tu- dar.de.sar- of.tǎ.dam/

I am in serious trouble!

اینقدر گُنده اش نکن! : ⓘ ✎

/in.ğadr- gon.de.aš- na.kon/

اینقدر گُندَش نکن! : ⓘ 💬

/in.ğadr- gon.daš- na.kon/

Don't make a big deal out of it!

از نگرانی دیشب خوابم نبُرد! : 💬 ✎

/az- ne.ga.rǎ.ni- di.šab- ǩǎ.bam- na.bord/

I was so worried that I couldn't sleep last night!

بیخودی نگرانی! : 💬 ✎

/bi.ǩo.di- ne.ga.rǎ.ni/

You're worried for no reason!

نمی دانم چرا نتیجه ی امتحان را اعلام نمی کنند! : ✎

/ne.mi.dǎ.nam- če.rǎ- na.ti.je.ye- em.te.hǎn- rǎ- e'.lǎm- ne.mi.ko.nand/

نمی دونم چرا نتیجه ی امتحانو اعلام نمی کنن! : 💬

/ne.mi.du.nam- če.rǎ- na.ti.je.ye- em.te.hǎ.no- e'.lǎm- ne.mi.ko.nan/

I don't know why they don't announce the exam's results!

صبر داشته باش. : 💬 ✎

/sabr- dǎš.te- bǎš/

Be patient!

✏️ ⓘ : این مشکل بدجوری گره خورده است!

/in- moš.kel- bad.ju.ri- ge.reh- ǩor.de- ast/

💬 ⓘ : این مشکل بدجوری گره خورده!

/in- moš.kel- bad- ju.ri- ge.re- ǩor.de/

This problem is a mess!

✏️ : غصّه نخور! حل می شود!

/ǧos.se- na.ǩor- hal- mi.ša.vad/

💬 : غصّه نخور! حل می شه!

/ǧos.se- na.ǩor- hal- mi.še/

Don't be so sad! It will be resolved!

✏️ ⓘ : نمی دانم دوباره می توانم یک روز رویِ پای خودم بایستم.

/ne.mi.dǎ.nam- do.bǎ.re- mi.ta.vǎ.nam- yek- ruz- ru.ye- pǎ.ye- ǩo.dam- be.is.tam/

💬 ⓘ : نمی دونم دوباره می تونم یه روز رویِ پای خودم وایسَم.

/ne.mi.du.nam- do.bǎ.re- mi.tu.nam- ye- ruz- ru.ye- pǎ.ye- ǩo.dam- vǎy.sam/

I don't know if I would be able to stand on my own feet again.

✏️ : معلوم است که می توانی.

/ma'.lum- ast- ke- mi.ta.vǎ.ni/

💬 : معلومه که می توونی.

/ma'.lu.me- ke- mi.tu.ni/

Of course you would.

139

Measurements

اندازه ی شلوارَت چیست؟ : ✏️

/an.dǎ.ze.ye- šal.vǎ.rat- čist/

اندازه ی شلوارت چیه؟ : 💬

/an.dǎ.ze.ye- šal.vǎ.ret- či.ye/

What size pants do you wear?

سی و دو. : 💬 ✏️

/si.yo- do/

Thirty two.

از این کت سایزِ بزرگ تر هم دارید؟ : ✏️

/az- in- kot- sǎy.ze- bo.zorg.tar- ham- dǎ.rid/

از این کت سایزِ بزرگ ترَم دارین؟ : 💬

/az- in- kot- sǎy.ze- bo.zorg.ta.ram- dǎ.rin/

Do you have this suit in a bigger size?

بله، داریم. : 💬 ✏️

/ba.le- dǎ.rim/

Yes we do.

✏️ : از این شلوار رنگ سیاهَش را هم دارید؟

/az- in- šal.vǎr- ran.ge- si.yǎ.haš- rǎ- ham- dǎ.rid/

💬 : از این شلوار رنگ سیاهش رو هم دارین؟

/az- in- šal.vǎr- ran.ge- si.yǎ.heš- ro- ham- dǎ.rin/

Do you have these pants in black?

💬 ✏️ : نه. متأسّفانه نداریم.

/na- mo.te.'as.se.fǎ.ne- na.dǎ.rim/

No. Unfortunately, we don't.

✏️ : شماره ی عینک شما چیست؟

/šo.mǎ.re.ye- 'ey.na.ke- šo.mǎ- čist/

💬 : شماره ی عینک تون چیه؟

/šo.mǎ.re.ye- 'ey.na.ke.tun- či.ye/

What strength are your glasses?

💬 ✏️ : یک، دوربین.

/yek- dur.bin/

1.00; far–sighted.

✏️ : آپارتمان شما چند مترست؟

/ǎ.pǎr.te.mǎ.ne- šo.mǎ- čand- met.rast/

💬 : آپارتمان تون چند متره؟

/ǎ.pǎr.te.mǎ.ne.tun- čand- met.re/

How many meters is your apartment?

💬 ✏️ : صد و بیست متر.

/sa.do- bist- metr/

One hundred and twenty meters.

✏️ : خانه ات چند اتاق دارد؟

/kǎ.ne.at- čand- o.tǎğ- dǎ.rad/

💬 : خونَت چند تا اتاق داره؟

/ku.nat- čand- tǎ- o.tǎğ- dǎ.re/

How many bedrooms does you house have?

💬 ✏️ : سه تا.

/se- tǎ/

Three.

✏️ : آپارتمانَت دو خوابه است یا سه خوابه؟

/ǎ.pǎr.te.mǎ.nat- do.kǎ.be- ast- yǎ- se.kǎ.be/

💬 : آپارتمانت دوخوابَس یا سه خوابه؟

/ǎ.pǎr.te.mǎ.net- do.kǎ.bas- yǎ- se.kǎ.be/

Is your apartment a two-bedroom or a three–bedroom?

💬 ✏️ : دو خوابه.

/do- kǎ.be/

Two-bedroom.

✏️ : شماره ی پای شما چندست؟

/šo.mǎ.re.ye- pǎ.ye- šo.mǎ- čan.dast/

💬 : شماره ی پاتون چنده؟

/šo.mǎ.re.ye- pǎ.tun- čan.de/

What size are your shoes?

💬 ✏️ : سی و هشت اروپا، هفت آمریکا.

/si.yo- haš.te- o.ru.pǎ- haf.te- ǎm.ri.kǎ/

Thirty eight European shoe size, seven American shoe size.

Measurements

✏️ : وزن شما چقدرست؟

/vaz.ne- šo.mǎ- če.ğad.rast/

💬 : وزن تون چقدره؟

/vaz.ne.tun- če.ğad.re/

How much do you weigh?

💬 ✏️ : صد و شصت پوند.

/sa.do- šast- pond/

One hundred and sixty pounds.

✏️ : قدّ شما چقدر است؟

/ğad.de- šo.mǎ- če.ğadr- ast/

💬 : قدّتون چقدره؟

/ğad.de.tun- če.ğad.re/

How tall are you?

💬 ✏️ : پنج فوت و ده اینچ.

/panj- fu.to- dah- inč/

Five feet and ten inches.

✏️ : چند کیلو وزن کم کرده ای؟

/čand- ki.lu- vazn- kam- kar.de.i/

💬 : چند کیلو وزن کم کردی؟

/čand- ki.lu- vazn- kam- kar.di/

How many kilos have you lost?

💬 ✏️ : دوازده کیلو.

/da.vǎz.dah- ki.lu/

Twelve kilos.

✏️ : چند پوند وزن اضافه کرده ای؟

/čand- pond- vazn- e.ză.fe- kar.de.i/

💬 : چند پوند وزن اضافه کردی؟

/čand- pond- vazn- e.ză.fe- kar.di/

How many pounds have you gained?

✏️💬 : نُه پوند.

/noh- pond/

Nine pounds.

✏️ : چند کیلو چاق شده ای؟

/čand- ki.lu- čăğ - šo.de.i/

💬 : چند کیلو چاق شدی؟

/čand- ki.lu- čăğ - šo.di/

How much weight have you gained?

✏️💬 : هفت – هشت کیلو.

/haft- hašt- ki.lu/

Seven to eight kilos.

✏️ : چند سانت قد کشیده ای؟

/čand- sănt- ğad- ke.ši.de.i/

💬 : چند سانت قد کشیدی؟

/čand- sănt- ğad- ke.ši.di/

How many centimeters have you grown?

✏️💬 : هفت سانت.

/haft- sănt/

Seven centimeters.

طول وَ عرضِ این قاب عکس چقدر است؟ : ✏️

/tul- va- 'ar.ze- in- ğă.be- 'aks- če.ğadr- ast/

طول و عرضِ این قاب عکس چقدره؟ : 💬

/tu.lo- 'ar.ze- in- ğă.be- 'aks- če.ğad.re/

What are this picture frame's measurements?

پنج سانت در ده سانت. : 💬 ✏️

/panj- sănt- dar- dah- sănt/

It's 5 by 10 cm.

عمقِ آن رودخانه چقدرست؟ : ✏️

/'om.ğe- ăn- rud.kă.ne- če.ğad.rast/

عمقِ اون رودخونه چقدره؟ : 💬

/'om.ğe- un- rud.ku.ne- če.ğad.re/

How deep is that river?

دو فوت. : 💬 ✏️

/do- fut/

Two feet.

145

Usages & Instructions

✏️ : اسمِ این چیست؟

/es.me- in- čist/

💬 : اسمِ این چیه؟

/es.me- in- či.ye/

What is it called?

💬 ✏️ : متّه ی برقی.

/mat.te.ye- bar.ği/

An electric drill.

✏️ : برایِ چه کاری ست؟

/ba.ră.ye- če- kă.rist/

💬 : برایِ چه کاریه؟

/ba.ră.ye - če- kă.ri.ye/

What is the purpose of this?

✏️ : برایِ سوراخ کردنِ دیوار است.

/ba.ră.ye- su.răk̆- kar.da.ne- di.văr- ast/

💬 : برایِ سوراخ کردنِ دیواره.

/ba.ră.ye- su.răk̆- kar.da.ne- di.vă.re/

It's for piercing the wall.

با این چه کار می کنند؟ : ✎
/bă- in- če- kăr- mi.ko.nand/

با این چی کار می کنن؟ : 💬
/bă- in- či- kăr- mi.ko.nan/

What do you do with this?

با این صفحه ی کامپیوتر را تمیز می کنند. : ✎
/bă- in- saf.he.ye- kăm.pi.yu.ter- ră- ta.miz- mi.ko.nand/

با این صفحه ی کامپیوترو تمیز می کنن. : 💬
/bă- in- saf.he.ye- kăm.pi.yu.te.ro- ta.miz- mi.ko.nan/

You clean the computer screen with this.

چطور کار می کند؟ : ✎
/in- če.tor- kăr- mi.ko.nad/

چطوری کار می کنه؟ : 💬
/in- če.to.ri- kăr- mi.ko.ne/

How does it work?

سیمِ آن را بکش! : ✎
/si.me- ăn- ră- be.keš/

سیمشو بکش! : 💬
/si.me.šo- be.keš/

Pull the string!

این به کامپیوترم می خورد؟ : ✎ ⓘ
/in- be- kăm.pi.yu.te.ram- mi.ǩo.rad/

این به کامپیوترم می خوره؟ : 💬 ⓘ
/in- be- kăm.pi.yu.te.ram- mi.ǩo.re/

Will it work with my computer?

دستورالعملَش را بخوان. : ✎
/das.tu.rol.'a.ma.laš- ră- be.ǩăn/

دستورِشو بخوون. : 💬
/das.tu.re.šo- be.ǩun/

Read the manual.

147

با این می شود دیوار را تمیز کرد؟ : ✏

/bă- in- mi.ša.vad- di.văr- ră- ta.miz- kard/

با این می شه دیوارو تمیز کرد؟ : 💬

/bă- in- mi.še- di.vă.ro- ta.miz- kard/

Can you clean the wall with this?

نه، روی قوطی اش نوشته است که فقط برای زمین است. : ✏

/na- ru.ye- ğu.ti.aš- ne.veš.te- ast- ke- fa.ğat- ba.ră.ye- za.min- ast/

نه، روی قوطیش نوشته فقط برای زمینه. : 💬

/na- ru.ye- ğu.tiš- ne.veš.te- fa.ğat- ba.ră.ye- za.mi.ne/

No. It says on the box that it's only for cleaning the floor.

این به چه دردی می خورد؟ : ① ✏

/in- be- če- dar.di- mi.ǩo.rad/

این به چه دردی می خوره؟ : ① 💬

/in- be- če- dar.di- mi.ǩo.re/

What is this good for?

این به درد پوست کندن سیب زمینی می خورد. : ① ✏

/in- be- dar.de- pust- kan.da.ne- sib.za.mi.ni- mi.ǩo.rad/

این به درد پوست کندن سیب زمینی می خوره. : ① 💬

/in- be- dar.de- pust- kan.da.ne- sib.za.mi.ni- mi.ǩo.re/

This is good for peeling potatoes.

این چطوری روشن می شود؟ : ✏

/in- če.to.ri- ro.šan- mi.ša.vad/

این چطوری روشن می شه؟ : 💬

/in- če.to.ri- ro.šan- mi.še/

How is it turned on?

دگمه ی بالای آن را فشار بده. : ✏

/dog.me.ye- bă.lă.ye- ăn- ră- fe.šăr- be.de/

دگمه ی بالاش رو فشار بده. : 💬

/dog.me.ye- bă.lăš- ro- fe.šăr- be.de/

Press the button on the top.

✏ : اوّل باید چه کار کنم؟

/av.val- bǎ.yad- če- kǎr- ko.nam/

💬 : اوّل باید چی کار کنم؟

/av.val- bǎ.yad- či- kǎr- ko.nam/

What should I do first?

✏ : بزنَش به برق.

/be.za.naš- be- barǧ/

💬 : بزنش به برق.

/be.za.neš- be- barǧ/

Plug it in.

✏ : این چطوری خاموش می شود؟

/in- če.to.ri- kǎ.muš- mi.ša.vad/

💬 : این چطوری خاموش می شه؟

/in- če.to.ri- kǎ.muš- mi.še/

How is it turned off?

✏ : سوئیچَش را بچرخان.

/su.ʻi.čaš- rǎ- be.čar.kǎn/

💬 : سوئیچشو بچرخون.

/su.ʻi.če.šo- be.čar.kun/

Turn the knob.

✏ : اشتباهَم کجاست؟

/eš.te.bǎ.ham- ko.jǎst/

💬 : اشتبام کجاس؟

/eš.te.bǎm- ko.jǎs/

What am I doing wrong?

✏ : نمی دانم. دوباره از اوّل شروع کن.

/ne.mi.dǎ.nam- do.bǎ.re- az- av.val- šo.ruʻ- kon/

💬 : نمی دونم. دوباره از اوّل شروع کن.

/ne.mi.du.nam- do.bǎ.re- az- av.val- šo.ruʻ- kon/

I don't know. Start over.

🖋 ⓘ : ازَش سر در نمی آورم.

/a.zaš- sar- dar- ne.mi.ă.va.ram/

💬 ⓘ : ارَش سر در نمیارم.

/a.zaš- sar- dar- ne.mi.yă.ram/

I can't figure it out.

🖋 ⓘ : چندبار تمرین کن، دستَت می آید.

/čand- băr- tam.rin- kon- das.tat- mi.ă.yad/

💬 ⓘ : چند بار تمرین کن، دستت میاد.

/čand- băr- tam.rin- kon- das.tet- mi.yăd/

Practice a couple of times; you'll get the hang of it.

🖋 : نمی توانم راهَش بیندازم.

/ne.mi.ta.vă.nam- ră.haš- bi.yan.dă.zam/

💬 : نمی تووم راش بندازم.

/ne.mi.tu.nam- răš- ben.dă.zam/

I can't seem to get this to work.

🖋 💬 : دوباره امتحان کن!

/do.bă.re- em.te.hăn- kon/

Try again!

🖋 : نمی توانم وصلَش کنم.

/ne.mi.ta.vă.nam- vas.laš- ko.nam/

💬 : نمی توونم وصلِش کنم.

/ne.mi.tu.nam- vas.leš- ko.nam/

I can't assemble it.

🖋 💬 : احتیاج به آچارِ مخصوص داری.

/eh.ti.yăj- be- ă.čă.re- maǩ.sus- dă.ri/

You need a special screwdriver.

150

Descriptions

3/29/22 Sneed

: ماشینَت چه رنگی است؟

/m.ši.nat- če- ran.gi- ast/

: ماشینت چه رنگیه؟

/m.ši.net- če- ran.gi.ye/

What color is your car?

: سیاه متالیک.

/si.yǎ.he- me.tǎ.lik/

Metallic black.

: این مدل رنگ های دیگر هم دارد؟

/in- mo.del- rang.hǎ.ye- di.gar- ham- dǎ.rad/

: این مدل رنگای دیگه هم داره؟

/in- mo.del- rangǎ.ye- di.ge- ham- dǎ.re/

Does this model come in other colors?

: بله. دو رنگ دیگر هم دارد: قرمز وَ سبز.

/ba.le- do- ran.ge- di.gar- ham- dǎ.rad- ğer.mez- va- sabz/

: بله. دو تا رنگ دیگه هم داره: قرمز و سبز.

/ba.le- do- ran.ge- di.ge- ham- dǎ.re- ğer.me.zo- sabz/

Yes. It comes in two other colors: red and green.

✏️ : چه شکلی ست؟

/če- šek.list/

💬 : چه شکلیه؟

/če- šek.li.ye/

What shape does it have?

✏️ : بیضی است.

/bey.zi- ast/

💬 : بیضیه.

/bey.zi.ye/

It's oval.

✏️ : شبیه به چیست؟

/ša.bih- be- čist/

💬 : شبیه چیه؟

/ša.bĩh- be- či.ye/

What does it look like?

✏️ : شبیه به سیب است.

/ša.bih- be- sib- ast/

💬 : شبیه سیبه.

/ša.bĩh- be- si.be/

It looks like an apple.

✏️ : جنسَش چیست؟

/jen.saš- čist/

💬 : جنسِش چیه؟

/jen.seš- či.ye/

What is it made of?

✏️ : آهنی است.

/ă.ha.nist/

💬 : آهنیه.

/ă.ha.ni.ye/

It's made of iron.

Descriptions

✏️ : شیشه ای ست یا پلاستیکی؟

/ši.še.ist- yǎ- pe.lǎs.ti.ki/

💬 : شیشه ایه یا پلاستیکی؟

/ši.še.i.ye- yǎ- pe.lǎs.ti.ki/

Is it made of glass or plastic?

✏️ : هیچکدام. فلزّی ست.

/hič.ko.dǎm- fe.lez.zist/

💬 : هیچکدوم. فلزّیه.

/hič.ko.dum- fe.lez.zi.ye/

Neither. It's made of metal.

✏️ : ساخت کجاست؟

/sǎk.te- ko.jǎst/

💬 : ساخت کجاس؟

/sǎk.te- ko.jǎs/

Where is it made?

✏️ : ساخت ژاپن است.

/sǎk.te- žǎ.pon- ast/

💬 : ساخت ژاپنه.

/sǎk.te- žǎ.po.ne/

It's made in Japan.

✏️ : این مارکَش چیست؟

/in- mǎr.kaš- čist/

💬 : این مارکِش چیه؟

/in- mǎr.keš- či.ye/

What is its brand?

✏️ : مارکَش معروف نیست.

/mǎr.kaš- maʾ.ruf- nist/

💬 : مارکِش معروف نیس.

/mǎr.keš- maʾ.ruf- nis/

It is not a brand name.

✏️ : کار دستّ است؟

/kǎ.re- dast- ast/

💬 : کار دسته؟

/kǎ.re- das.te/

Is it hand–made?

✏️ : نه. ماشینی است.

/na- mǎ.ši.ni- ast/

💬 : نه. ماشینیه.

/na- mǎ.ši.ni.ye/

No. It's machine–made.

✏️ : ضدّ آب است؟

/zed.de- ǎb- ast/

💬 : ضدّ آبه؟

/zed.de- ǎ.be/

Is it waterproof?

✏️ : نه. امّا ضدّ ضربه است.

/na- am.mǎ- zed.de- zar.be- ast/

💬 : نه. امّا ضدّ ضربَس.

/na- am.mǎ- zed.de- zar.bas/

No, but it's shockproof.

✏️ : این را می شود در ماشین ظرفشویی گذاشت؟

/in- rǎ- mi.ša.vad- dar- mǎ.ši.ne- zarf.šu.yi- go.zǎšt/

💬 : اینو میشه تو ماشین ظرفشویی گذاشت؟

/i.no- mi.še- tu- mǎ.ši.ne- zarf.šu.yi- go.zǎšt/

Is this a dishwasher safe item?

✏️ : آره، امّا در ماکروویو نمی شود گذاشت.

/ǎ.re- am.mǎ- dar- mǎk.ro.veyv- ne.mi.ša.vad- go.zǎšt/

💬 : آره، امّا توی ماکروویو نمی شه گذاشت.

/ǎ.re- am.mǎ- tu.ye- mǎk.ro.veyv- ne.mi.še- go.zǎšt/

Yes, but it is not microwavable.

✎ : جنسَش خوب است؟

/jen.saš- ǩub- ast/

💬 : جنسش خوبه؟

/jen.seš- ǩu.be/

Is it made of good material?

✎ : بله. کیفیتَش بالاست.

/ba.le- key.fi.ya.taš- bă.lăst/

💬 : بله. کیفیتش بالاس.

/ba.le- key.fi.ya.teš- bă.lăs/

Yes. It is made of high quality material.

✎ : آخرین مدل است؟

/ă.ǩa.rin- mo.del- ast/

💬 : آخرین مدله؟

/ă.ǩa.rin- mo.de.le/

Is it the latest model?

✎ : بله. تازه وارد بازار شده است.

/ba.le- tă.ze- vă.re.de- bă.zăr- šo.de- ast/

💬 : بله. تازه اومده تو بازار.

/ba.le- tă.ze- u.ma.de- tu- bă.zăr/

Yes. It's new to the market.

✎ : تازه در آمده است؟

/tă.ze- dar- ă.ma.de- ast/

💬 : تازه در اومده؟

/tă.ze- dar- u.ma.de/

Is it a new release?

✎ : نه، قدیمی است.

/na- ğa.di.mi- ast/

💬 : نه، قدیمیه.

/na- ğa.di.mi.ye/

No. It's old.

✎ : جنسَش بدست؟
/jen.saš- ba.dast/

💬 : جنسش بده؟
/jen.̄seš- ba.de/

Is it made of poor material?

✎ : خیلی بُنجل است.
/ǩey.li- bon.jol- ast/

💬 : خیلی بُنجله.
/ǩey.li- bon.jo.le/

It is made of very cheap material.

✎ : دَوامَش خوب است؟
/da.vǎ.maš- ǩub- ast/

💬 : دَوومش خوبه؟
/da.vu.̄meš- ǩu.be/

Is it durable?

✎ : نه، زود می شکند.
/n̄a- zud- mi.še.ka.nad/

💬 : نه، زود می شکنه.
/na- zud- miš.ka.ne/

No. It breaks easily.

💬 : ازَش راضی هستی؟
/a.zaš- rǎ.zi- has.ti/

Are you happy with it?

✎ : نه. پول دور ریختن است.
/na- pul- dur- riǩ.tan- ast/

💬 : نه. پول دور ریختنه.
/na- pul- dur- riǩ.ta.ne/

No. It's a waste of money.

Descriptions

✏️ : جارو برقی تازه ات چطورست؟

/jă.ru.bar.ği.ye- tă.ze.at- če.to.rast/

💬 : جارو برقی تازَت چطوره؟

/jă.ru.bar.ği.ye- tă.zat- če.to.re/

How is your new vacuum cleaner?

✏️ : خیلی بدست! آشغال است!

/ǩey.li- ba.dast- ăš.ğăl- ast/

💬 : خیلی بده! آشغاله!

/ǩey.li- ba.de- ăš.ğă.le/

Horrible! It's a piece of junk.

✏️ : لوکس است؟

/luks- ast/

💬 : لوکسه؟

/luk.se/

Is it top-of-the-line?

✏️ : نه، امّا تا مدّت ها کار می کند.

/na- am.mă- tă- mod.dat.hă- kăr- mi.ko.nad/

💬 : نه، امّا حالا حالاها کار می کنه.

/na- am.mă- hă.lă- hă.lă.hă- kăr- mi.ko.ne/

No, but it will work for a long time.

✏️ : خوب تمیز می کند؟

/ǩub- ta.miz- mi.ko.nad/

💬 : خوب تمیز می کنه؟

/ǩub- ta.miz- mi.ko.ne/

Does it clean well?

ⓘ ✏️ : معجزه می کند!

/mo'.je.ze- mi.ko.nad/

ⓘ 💬 : معجزه می کنه!

/mo'.je.ze- mi.ko.ne/

It works miracles!

🖊 ⌨ : از کجا خریدی؟

/az- ko.jă- ǩa.ri.di/

Where did you buy this?

🖊 : بیشتر فروشگاه ها دارند.

/biš.ta.re- fo.ruš.gǎh.hǎ- dǎ.rand/

⌨ : بیشتر فروشگاها دارن.

/biš.ta.re- fo.ruš.gǎ.hǎ- dǎ.ran/

Most stores have it.

🖊 : این را چطور می شود خرید؟

/in- rǎ- če.tor- mi.ša.vad- ǩa.rid/

⌨ : اینو چطوری می شه خرید؟

/i.no- če.to.ri- mi.še- ǩa.rid/

How can I buy this?

🖊 : باید سفارش ویژه بدهی.

/bǎ.yad- se.fǎ.re.še- vi.že- be.da.hi/

⌨ : باید سفارش ویژه بدی.

/bǎ.yad- se.fǎ.re.še- vi.že- be.di/

It's a special order.

Prices & Costs

✏️ : این بلوز چندست؟

/in- bo.luz- čan.dast/

💬 : این بلوز چنده؟

/in- bo.luz- čan.de/

How much is this shirt?

✏️💬 : سی دلار.

/si- do.lăr/

Thirty dollars.

✏️ : شهریه ی کلاس زبان فارسی چقدرست؟

/šah.ri.ye.ye- ke.lǎ.se- za.bǎ.ne- fǎr.si- če.ğad.rast/

💬 : شهریه ی کلاس زبان فارسی چقدره؟

/šah.ri.ye.ye- ke.lǎ.se- za.bǎ.ne- fǎr.si- če.ğad.re/

How much is the tuition for the Persian class?

✏️ : نمی دانم، امّا باید گران باشد.

/ne.mi.dǎ.nam- am.mǎ- bǎ.yad- ge.rǎn- bǎ.šad/

💬 : نمی دونم، امّا باید گرون باشه.

/ne.mi.du.nam- am.mǎ- bǎ.yad- ge.run- bǎ.še/

I don't know, but it should be expensive.

✎ : کرایه ی اتوبوس چقدرست؟

/ke.rǎ.ye.ye- o.to.bus- če.ğad.rast/

💬 : کرایه ی اتوبوس چقدره؟

/ke.rǎ.ye.ye- o.to.bus- če.ğad.re/

How much is the bus fare?

✎ : باید بپرسم، امّا قاعدتاً نباید زیاد باشد.

/bǎ.yad- be.por.sam- am.mǎ- ğǎ.'e.da.tan- na.bǎ.yad- zi.yǎd- bǎ.šad/

💬 : باید بپرسم، امّا قاعدتاً نباید زیاد باشه.

/bǎ.yad- be.por.sam- am.mǎ- ğǎ.'e.da.tan- na.bǎ.yad- zi.yǎd- bǎ.še/

I have to ask, but it can't be much.

✎ : ماشین تان را چند خریدید؟

/mǎ.ši.ne.tǎn- rǎ- čand- ǩa.ri.did/

💬 : ماشین تونو چند خریدین؟

/mǎ.ši.ne.tu.no- čand- ǩa.ri.din/

How much did you pay for your car?

✎ : گران نخریدیم. دست دوّم است.

/ge.rǎn- na.ǩa.ri.dim- das.te- dov.vom- ast/

💬 : گرون نخریدیم. دست دوّمه.

/ge.run- na.ǩa.ri.dim- das.te- dov.vo.me/

It wasn't expensive. It's used.

✎ ⓘ : چقدر برایَت تمام شد؟

/če.ğadr- ba.rǎ.yat- ta.mǎm- šod/

💬 ⓘ : چقدر برات تموم شد؟

/če.ğadr- ba.rǎt- ta.mum- šod/

How much did it cost you?

💬 ✎ : هیچّی. مجّانّی بود.

/hič.či- maj.jǎ.ni- bud/

Zero. It was free.

✏️ : قیمتَش چندست؟

/ğey.ma.taš- čan.dast/

💬 : قیمتش چنده؟

/ğey.ma.teš- čan.de/

What's the price?

✏️ 💬 : دویست هزار دلار.

/de.vist- he.zăr- do.lăr/

Two hundred thousand dollars.

ⓘ ✏️ : خیلی بالایَش پول دادی؟

/ḱey.li- bă.lă.yaš- pul- dă.di/

ⓘ 💬 : خیلی بالاش پول دادی؟

/ḱey.li- bă.lăš- pul- dă.di/

Did you pay a lot for it?

✏️ : نه. ارزان بود.

/na- ar.zăn- bud/

💬 : نه. ارزون بود.

/na- ar.zun- bud/

No, it was inexpensive.

✏️ : نمی دانم این کیف را بخرم یا نخرم.

/ne.mi.dă.nam- in- kif- ră- be.ḱa.ram- yă- na.ḱa.ram/

💬 : نمی دونم این کیفو بخرم یا نخرم.

/ne.mi.du.nam- in- ki.fo- be.ḱa.ram- yă- na.ḱa.ram/

I don't know if I should buy this bag or not.

✏️ : حتماً بخر. مُفت است.

/hat.man- be.ḱar- moft- ast/

💬 : حتماً بخر. مُفته.

/hat.man- be.ḱar- mof.te/

You should definitely buy it. It's a bargain.

✏ : فکر می کنی به قیمتَش می ارزد؟

/fekr- mi.ko.ni- be- ğey.ma.taš- mi.ar.zad/

💬 : فکر می کنی به قیمتش میارزه؟

/fekr- mi.ko.ni- be- ğey.ma.teš- mi.yar.ze/

Do you think it is worth the money?

✏ : نه. بیخودی گران است.

/na- bi.ǩo.di- ge.rǎn- ast/

💬 : نه. بیخودی گرونه.

/na- bi.ǩo.di- ge.ru.ne/

No. It's overpriced.

✏ : قیمتَش مناسب است؟

/ğey.ma.taš- mo.nǎ.seb- ast/

💬 : قیمتش مناسبه؟

/ğey.ma.teš- mo.nǎ.se.be/

Is it affordable?

✏ : نه گران است، نه ارزان.

/na- ge.rǎn- ast- na- ar.zǎn/

💬 : نه گرونه، نه ارزون.

/na- ge.ru.ne- na- ar.zun/

It's just the right price.

✏ : میزتان را چقدر خوب خریده اید!

/mi.ze.tǎn- rǎ- če.ğadr- ǩub- ǩa.ri.de.id/

💬 : میزتون رو چقدر خوب خریدین!

/mi.ze.tu.no- če.ğadr- ǩub- ǩa.ri.din/

You bought your table at such a good price!

✏ : آره، شانس آوَردیم. حراج بود.

/ǎ.re- šǎns- ǎ.var.dim- ha.rǎj- bud/

💬 : آره، شانس آوُردیم. حراج بود.

/ǎ.re- šǎns- ǎ.vor.dim- ha.rǎj- bud/

Yes, we were lucky. It was on sale.

✎ 💬 : قیمتِ این کتاب چند بود؟

/ğey.ma.te- in- ke.tăb- čand- bud/

What was the price of this book?

✎ 💬 : با بیست درصد تخفیف، پنج دلار.

/bă- bist- dar.sad- tak̆.fif- panj- do.lăr/

With the twenty percent discount, it was five dollars.

163

INDEX OF IDIOMS, EXPRESSIONS AND SLANG
USED IN THIS BOOK

از هر پنجه ی کسی صد هنر ریختن

to have numerous skills and talents

Example:

پسرم از هر پنجه اش صد هنر می ریزد. گیتار می زند، نقّاشی می کند، آشپزی اش هم عالی ست.

My son has so many talents. He plays guitar, paints and cooks like a pro.

اعصابِ کسی را بهم ریختن

to get on someone's nerves/ to exhaust someone mentally or emotionally

Example:

نمی توانم کار پیدا کنم. این مشکل بدجوری اعصابم را به هم ریخته است.

I can't find a job. This problem has gotten on my nerves.

با کسی بهم زدن

to break up with someone

Example:

من با دوست پسرم بهم زدم.

I broke up with my boyfriend.

بالای چیزی پول دادن

to pay for an item

Example:

من خیلی بالای این ماشین پول داده ام.

I've paid way too much for this car.

به چیزی امید بستن

to have one's hopes up

Example:

امید بسته بودم که امسال خانه می خریم.

I had my hopes up that we would buy a house this year.

به چیزی(غذایی) لب نزدن 98

not to be able to touch food

Example:

آنقدر خسته بودم که به غذایم لب نزدم.

I was so tired that I didn't touch my food.

به خود رسیدن 54

to take care of one's appearance

Example:

من همیشه به خودم می رسم.

I always take care of my appearance.

به دستِ کسی آمدن 191

to get the hang of something

Example:

چند بار امتحان کردم تا دستم آمد که چطوری کار می کند.

I tried a couple of times and I got the hang of how it worked.

به دل بد آوردن 173

to worry for no reason/ to anticipate a bad ending for something

Example:

خوب نیست بی دلیل به دلت بد بیاوری.

It's not a good thing to worry too much for no reason.

به سرِ کسی زدن 69

to think of doing something unplanned/ to come up with a sudden decision

Example:

به سرم زده است از شغلم استعفا بدهم!

I'm thinking about quitting my job!

به کسی برخوردن
to get offended

Example:

به من برخورد که جواب تلفنم را ندادی.

I got offended that you didn't answer my call.

پدر کسی درآمدن
to have a hell of a time

Example:

پدرمان درآمد تا زیرزمین تمیز شد!

We had a hell of a time before the basement was cleaned.

توی خود بودن
to be unusually quiet and preoccupied, not to be oneself

Example:

امروز خیلی توی خودت هستی!

You are too quiet today!

توی دردسر افتادن
to be in trouble

Example:

اگر زنم من را ببیند توی دردسر می افتم.

If my wife sees me, I will be in trouble.

جان کسی به لبش رسیدن
to be fed up with something

Example:

از دست صاحبخانه ام جانم به لبم رسیده است.

I'm fed up with my landlord's behavior.

چشم های کسی برق زدن

for someone's eyes to sparkle

Example:

از خوشحالی چشم هایت برق می زنند.

Your eyes are sparkling from happiness.

چیزی برای چیزی جان دادن

for something to call for or be perfect for something

Example:

این پالتو جان می دهد برای روزهای سرد زمستانی.

This coat is great for the cold wintry days.

چیزی برای کسی تمام شدن

to cost someone something

Example:

کلاس فارسی برایم خیلی گران تمام شد.

The Persian class cost me a lot of money.

چیزی به چیزی خوردن

for something to work with or be compatible with something

Example:

این کلید به آن قفل نمی خورد.

This key doesn't work with that lock.

چیزی به درد چیزی (کاری/کسی) خوردن

for something to be good for something or someone

Example:

این کتاب خیلی به درد من می خورد.

I have a very good use for this book.

چیزی به ذهنِ کسی رسیدن

to be reminded of something/ to come up with an idea, a plan, etc

Example:

دیشب ایده ی جالبی به ذهنم رسید.

Last night I came up with a great idea.

چیزی به کسی آمدن

for something to suit someone very well

Example:

این لباس خیلی به تو می آید.

This dress suits you very well.

چیزی به کسی چسبیدن

to enjoy something very much

Example:

آتش بازی خیلی به بچّه ها چسبید.

The kids enjoyed the fireworks a lot.

چیزی به کسی مزه کردن

to enjoy eating/drinking something

Example:

بستنی توی این هوایِ گرم خیلی به ما مزه کرد.

We enjoyed having ice cream in this hot weather.

چیزی (مراسمی) بهم خوردن

for an event, arrangement to be canceled

Example:

جشنِ تولّدم بهم خورد.

My birthday party was canceled.

دخلِ کسی آمدن

to be the end of someone/ to go to hell and back

Example:

دخلم آمد تا ده پوند وزن کم کردم.

I went to hell and back before I lost ten pounds.

دست پختِ کسی حرف نداشتن

for someone's cooking to be flawless

Example:

همه می دانند که من دست پختم حرف ندارد.

Everybody knows that my cooking is perfect.

دستِ کسی درد نکردن

to hope someone is not tired after doing you a favor/ a phrase used to thank someone for their service

Example:

دستت درد نکند! چقدر لباس قشنگی برای من دوخته ای!

I hope you're not exhausted! What a beautiful dress you've made for me!

دلِ کسی برای چیزی (کسی) تنگ شدن

to miss someone

Example:

دلم برای مادرم تنگ شده است.

I missed my mother.

دماغِ کسی سوختن

to be bummed out

Example:

فکر کردم در مسابقه برنده می شوم اما باختم! دماغم سوخت!

I thought I would win the competition but I lost! I was bummed out!

دنیا به آخر رسیدن

to be the end of the world

Example:

اگر امروز سر کار نروی، دنیا به آخر نمی رسد.

It's not going to be the end of the world if you don't go to work today!

راهی (راهِ حلّی) جلوی پای کسی گذاشتن

to give someone advice to solve a problem

Example:

راهی که جلوی پایت می گذارم، بهترین راه است.

My suggestion to you is the best way to solve this problem.

روی پای خود ایستادن

to stand on your own feet/ to become independent

Example:

می خواهم هرچه زودتر روی پای خودم بایستم.

I want to stand on my own feet as soon as possible.

زحمت کشیدن

to work very hard

Example:

من برای فروشِ این خانه خیلی زحمت کشیدم.

I worked very hard to sell this house.

کارِ کسی گرفتن

to run a business successfully

Example:

برادرم رستوران باز کرده است و کارش خیلی گرفته است.

My brother opened a restaurant and it is doing great.

173

کسی را از پا در آوردن

to make someone extremely exhausted

Example:

این بیماری من را از پا در آورد.

This illness has exhausted me tremendously.

126

کمکی (کاری) از دست کسی برآمدن

to be able to do something for someone or to help someone

Example:

دکترها می گویند هیچ کاری از دست شان برنمی آید.

The doctors say there is nothing they can do.

177

کاری (مشکلی) گره خوردن

a problem being too difficult to be resolved

Example:

کار مهاجرت من گره خورده است.

My immigration situation is a mess.

20

کسی را به جا آوردن

to recognize someone

Example:

من اصلاً پدرت را به جا نیاوردم.

I didn't recognize your father at all.

130

کسی را به زحمت انداختن

to trouble someone

Example:

نمی خواستم کسی را به زحمت بیندازم.

I didn't want to trouble anyone.

130

نوشِ جان!

Enjoy!

Example:

نوشِ جانِ تان، هر چقدر می خواهید بخورید.

Enjoy! Eat as much as you want.

175

همین است که هست!

It is what it is!

Example:

چه خوشت بیاید چه نیاید، باید قبولش کنی. همین است که هست!

Like it or not, you have to accept this. It is what it is!

Similar Titles

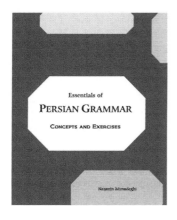

Essentials of
Persian Grammar:
Concepts and Exercises
Nazanin Mirsadeghi

Laugh and Learn
Persian Idioms
Nazanin Mirsadeghi

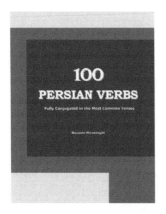

100
Persian Verbs
(Fully Conjugated in the Most Common Tenses)
Nazanin Mirsadeghi

1000 +
Most Useful
Persian Words
Nazanin Mirsadeghi

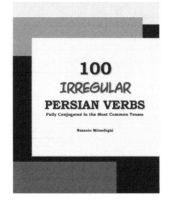

100
Irregular
Persian Verbs
(Fully Conjugated in the Most Common Tenses)
Nazanin Mirsadeghi

Persian Folktale

**Once Upon a Time
(Seven Persian Folktales)**
Persian/Farsi Edition
Meimanat Mirsadeghi (Zolghadr)

To Learn More About BAHAR BOOKS

Please Visit the Website :

Bahar Books

www.baharbooks.com

Made in United States
Orlando, FL
21 March 2022

15986305R00100